A Corrected Economic Republic

-Adam D. Vass Gal

Table of Contents

Preface

The *idea* of *America* is becoming a gentler, kinder, and more international version of its original form. We are adopting many European ideals and escalating our popularity all over the world. Some of the damage to our reputation created during the previous administration is being healed and even the Middle East appears to being opening up to the *New America* of today. We now have the first African-American president in our history and have just passed universal healthcare in an effort to provide a service that has been neglected in this country for far too long. However, we are also dealing blow after blow to the strongest economy in the world, and these shots could not be more devastating if they were delivered by a world-class boxer.

The U.S. government has historically been strong for a couple of reasons. Number one is that we were a nation formed by people with an adventurous spirit and a faith in both God and their ability to turn hard work into results. The early pioneers left their respective countries to come to the new world to drop the chains of an oppressive government for the promise of a freedom that is provided only when coupled with personal responsibility. They knew that once they arrived, the sky was the limit and there were no safety nets. It was a work or perish situation and the "necessity is the mother of invention" philosophy led our hard working nation to unmatched riches.

The Chinese have a saying, "wealth does not pass three generations." The three generations are characterized by wealth accumulation, wealth preservation, and wealth destruction. As a nation, there is a strong possibility that we are moving out of the accumulation stage and into preservation. Our leaders and the majority of our voters have determined that our original fighting spirit is gone and that the citizens who have money will always have it and should support those who choose not to fight for themselves. Winston Churchill said that "Socialism is a philosophy of failure, the creed of ignorance, and the gospel of envy, its inherit virtue is the equal sharing of misery." It is clearly a method of preserving wealth with one fateful twist: socialism divides the care of said wealth between the people that made it and the people that did not.

The step to preservation is a sad one; it is the tale of one who has hit the lottery or received some kind of unexpected inheritance. They shut down the spirited pursuit of a better life and adamantly move toward protecting what they have at the moment. The person who takes this step has told the world and perhaps themselves that they are now incapable of moving themselves forward and have become dependent on tangible objects rather than their own drive, initiative, and grit. The loss of these ideals among the American people is a depressing state of affairs and a clear indicator of our progression into the second generation.

We need to find a way to move back to the fundamentals that spawned our nation. It is time to take a more classical look at the economy and the proper role of our government. The problems that we have today need to be addressed and the inherent flaws in our fiscal and monetary policy need to be corrected or eliminated. Our contemporary government is mature enough to determine which economic matrices work, which ones do not, and which ones cause irreparable damage. My love for this country and economic study have given me a strong sense of what is fundamentally right and what is going to be a poison. We are dangerously close to forming a nation that will be unable to correct its wayward path.

Chapter 1:

Societal Flaws and Changes in the Electorate

The successful measure of any nation starts with its government and the structure that is used to make the country run. One can easily argue that the United States is neither the smartest nation, nor is it blessed with unequaled natural resources. We have no other significant advantage over the rest of the world aside from one exception—our economic structure. The ability to let the free market work and flourish makes addressing issues that need attention a way of life. We see problems as opportunities because that is what they are in a free market. To identify a shortcoming and perfect its improvement is what allows an American to separate himself from the herd socially and financially.

This brings up a fundamental question for any nation. What is the role of our government? A government's role can be at least categorized into two divisions—productive and protective. The protective role is important and can offer a direct relationship between work and reward. The military is an alternative to any young man or woman. It does not discriminate unless you are physically unable to handle the work. You can pull yourself out of any condition and make something of your life on the basis of your heart and character. This sounds like a wonderful opportunity and it is. Still, many see it as an unattractive option when compared to sitting at home while receiving a government check that offers pay raises outpacing military income each year. You can unfortunately see the validity of such a decision.

"Idle hands are the devil's workshop" is another truism. Much of the gang related activity in this country should be replaced by the severe discipline of the military. The willingness of young men and women to adopt a gang lifestyle comes from hopeless living conditions and their perceived lack of attractive opportunities. When a means is provided by the government to any member of society to avoid work, it can only result in dangerous consequences. The secret seems to be correlating pay with work. If you do not work, then you do not get paid.

We have accepted an entirely different approach to dealing with this situation. Our government pays a person to not work. We pay people who cannot afford children to have more children. When incentive is eliminated, initiative goes with it. The worst part of this whole situation is the absence of shame for people on welfare. It is a source of pride in some odd ways and even food stamps are being offered through a debit card; so that the stigma of using stamps is eliminated. There are certainly those who warrant some assistance and I am not addressing people with disabilities who legitimately need help. Though, many people on welfare do not fall into this category. They make ignorant, yet selfish decisions to increase their monthly pay and, at times, take pride in that system. This culture of willing dependency has now evolved to the point that an individual will often attempt to degrade anyone who tries to rise above it and work toward a better life.

Our government makes decisions based on maintaining popularity and retaining voters. This survival instinct affects every piece of legislation and corrupts the decision making process. It would seem appropriate to create bills that cater to the people and their wants, but the short and long-term costs must always be accounted for before a final decision is made. We have started down a dangerous road of paying for voters. Our politicians not only pay back the contributors that put them into office, but they increase national spending in ways that will repay them with future voters. Improper government efforts are extremely dangerous when offered through the electoral system.

Funding needs to be disconnected from decision-making. We need to find a better format with which to build our collective leadership. Having just two parties no longer provides the level of competition needed to correctly run the most powerful economy in the world. We have one side that is pushing for legislation that will socialize everything that is challenging for the average citizen to attain, while the wealthy foot the bill. The other side has become so disgusted with this motive that they clamp down even tighter on the money they have created and saved. Both major parties continue to grow apart at the expense of the American people.

A political system should be created to elect a better president; one which takes into account leadership roles, education, and business experience. These people should then be approached about the opportunity to run for President of the United States. It would really be something to see men and women looking to fill this position who are truly impressive in both their background and career accomplishments. This screening effort would bring forth the cream of the crop for a job that deserves just such a person. Many of these people would probably take a pay cut to be the President, but I do believe that the combination of an accomplished man or woman with the civic pride to make such a sacrifice is a perfect candidate.

Once the pre-screening is completed and the top 100 candidates are chosen (two from each state), let the American people start to weed out the candidates they do not like. I am not proposing an *American Idol* style election process, but the first cut could come from the representatives of each state.

They would narrow the list to 20 candidates who will then go through a series of interviews that would be nationally televised. This would lead to a national vote to narrow the field to five people (somewhat akin to the primaries). The final stage would involve a series of debates and town hall meetings which would ultimately provide the people enough information to make a decision on whom they would want to lead the country. There would be no campaigning or money spent on the electoral process outside of the stages described previously and possibly a new suit. Our present system's tendency to allow individual (and party) wealth to determine leadership needs to cease.

Promised income and indefinable benefits determining leadership also needs to end. If one receives government assistance, then that person should forfeit his or her right to vote. That is the only way to disconnect voting from government spending. The conflict of interest in this area is too great and must be eliminated. Voting for a candidate based on the amount of assistance that you will receive from that person is immoral, selfish, irresponsible, and happening at an increasing rate. Another side effect of this movement would be the creation of a new sense of pride in all citizens. Hopefully, giving away one of your most sacred rights as an American would not be taken lightly. It would also prompt one, perhaps, to ensure such a monumental loss only temporarily. Once you get back on your feet and leave the public assistance program you are using, you regain the right to vote. The goal is temporary assistance over a cradle to grave system.

Government intervention must decrease. It needs to provide only to the disabled and to those who give something in return. If we cannot get through the consumption-payment disconnect, then our economy will be in real trouble. We need protection from other countries, fires, and those who break the law. These are valid expenses for tax payer money. We have lost our sense of responsibility for the proper use of someone's hard earned cash. It is taken for granted and, like most conditions removed from the free market, it is wasted.

The degree of any country's economic freedom was the exact degree of its progress. America, the freest, achieved the most.

      -Ayn Rand

Chapter 2:

Government Structure and Oversight of the States

A government cannot run correctly or build upon itself following each election cycle if predetermined requirements are not in place for exactly what the country's leadership should provide. The first requirement needs to be the passage of—and adherence to--a balanced budget. Borrowing results in waste. Today, the American national debt has caused an annual interest expense that is continually growing and could eventually rival our spending on Social Security, military, or welfare. Paying interest only on the national debt is equivalent to making minimum payments on a credit card. It builds the debt and creates a hole that grows deeper each year, destroying both nations and households in equal measure. The correction to this would be to address the few issues that need to be covered by the tax payers, cut the unnecessary expenses, and pay down the debt. When this is completed, the government should lower taxes.

What gets cut? Unfortunately, this is a tedious process and must be addressed issue by issue. I will point out a few major ones, but the minor ones have the same cumulative effect. Still, the answer comes more from looking at the programs that do not get cut. The military, the police, the fire departments, the care of our truly disabled, and the maintenance of roads, and parks cover most of what the taxpayers should support. These are necessities that cannot be properly provided in the private sector for logistical, safety, or other complications. I am not completely against taxes because it is a small reflection of one's commitment to this country. I do despise tax abuse though and we are a long way from only covering the essentials.

Why the waste? There are several reasons. The first is the failed economic theories of John Maynard Keynes. I don't personally blame Keynes for the budget and structural problems in the United States because we are, of course, using only the parts of Keynesian economics that suit the current leaders in office. For example, his management of an economy proposes that nations cut taxes and increase government spending during difficult times. This is supposed to spur spending and economic growth. We have no trouble following through with this part; yet, he also suggests that a government cut its spending and raise taxes during economic booms to make up for the earlier created deficit.

There are a couple of flaws with this step. The first is that you are not always assured to have a boom that can accommodate the earlier spending and will risk turning a temporary deficit into permanent debt. The second issue is with raising taxes. We have automatic stabilizers in our system that take affect without legislation, such as progressive income taxing. As income increases, more tax revenue is sent to our government at a progressive rate. However, if funds need to be raised, we cannot do it. We refuse to cut our unnecessary programs that were started to help during recessions and we refuse to raise taxes. The reason: Neither of these actions gets a politician reelected. It is clear that Keynes ignored the human condition and that was a critical mistake. Sometimes, ideas work well on paper, but they fail in implementation. This is the case with Keynes.

There is an expression used in the South that has an individual jokingly say, "I only know enough to be dangerous." The harsh reality of this statement is that many of our politicians have this relationship with economic policy. They quote great thinkers and loosely interpret their ideas, but tragically fail with their implementation because they only know enough to be dangerous. Economists should be used to sculpt economic policy. The policy needs to be outlined and enacted to total completion. Taking the bits and pieces that satisfy voters without the critical budgeting and fund raising necessary to keep balance creates a cancer for any nation. The cancers of our nation seem to grow every year and one may wonder if we can ever recover.

The reason we are in this situation is because the U.S. government has moved away from its protective function into a hybrid government that goes beyond guarding freedoms by the defense of the military and the establishment of personal rights. It is branching into every area of our lives through the economy and through its intrusion into making decisions that can only be established by moral foundation. It is amazing how difficult the federal government has made such a simple concept. The duty of the United States to her people is to guard against intruders, promote competition, and protect individual rights. That is it. Taxes should be minimal and only exist for these basic needs. The government is not a conduit that serves to simply move money from the people that earn it to the people that do not. The federal government would serve better by taking a step back, loosening its grip, and by letting the states handle moral issues that do not interfere with another individual's personal rights. The government should take the approach of a good baseball hitter holding the bat. Loosen your grip and then loosen it again!

It may be because I am a lifelong Southerner that I am an advocate of a state's right to make decisions about the laws that govern its citizens. This notion would make the federal government fall more to a secondary role that covers only interstate issues. I believe that the market is pushing our predominately capitalist society to this natural division of oversight. The federal government should set rules for anything that covers commerce and the states should handle social and moral decisions. Values and religion would be a more common debate at the state level whereas economic and international views would be more appropriate for a presidential discussion.

State regulation in regard to commerce can be an issue and an easy example of that is the insurance industry. There are barriers to entry, complications with coverage across state lines, and limitations to competition. Despite living in such an information friendly society, we also aggressively regulate several of our everyday communication mediums. With state-regulated insurance, a sale must take place in that state and the insurer must be licensed in that state. No faxing, e-mailing, or scanning can bridge the geographical gap. Furthermore, two parties can only do business in the state from which the seller resides and if the client lives in another state, then they must be licensed in each additional state. It is entirely too complicated and it covers all insurance sales, including annuities.

States need to be more focused on running their own governments and addressing moral decisions and topics. Gay marriage, abortion, and other emotionally-charged social issues should be determined by each state. Different areas will have different values and that can be reflected in how they choose to govern their people. If a state wants to offer gay marriage, then they should be able to do so (of course, I am a proponent of the government not having any hand in marriage, but let us move one step at a time). It certainly does not hurt anyone and if the state's voters are fine with the moral side of that debate, then there should not be a problem with the decision. If a state feels that they do not support abortion, then they should have the right to disallow that practice inside of their borders.

This will create a more efficient government process in the future. A state will be able to decide if it would like to be more progressive when it comes to science. They can look into stem cell research, animal experimentation, green initiatives, and cloning. These choices are based on a moral foundation that might be different depending on the region. The government should exist to allow free choice right up to the point where someone's free choice starts to infringe on another person. If a state wants to allow a certain area of science that is not open to other municipalities, then that state will start to connect researchers who share a common discipline. This arrangement will allow science to flourish in spite of religion and opposing ethical views.

This division of regulation will protect all minorities--not just racially, but through a common sharing of beliefs. As diverse as the United States is, we still attempt to make decisions on topics that have no business being in front of a judge on the federal level. The government's role needs to be small and protective in nature. Each state has a more appropriate duty to maintain the moral foundation of its people. Of course, not everyone shares the same beliefs even at the state level. Conversely, you can certainly find a much greater commonality between people populating a smaller region. There are several issues right now that can be very different as you cross state lines. Abortion, capital punishment, and gay marriage are all determined at the state level as they should be.

The major transition will be moving the states away from regulating trade. All trade needs to be monitored at the federal level. The American economy is far too big to attempt an oversight of commerce by separate parties that may have different rules. It only limits the potential of transactions and develops monopolies. Free trade can be achieved only when barriers are knocked down and restrictions are eliminated that pertain to geographic location. Agencies that cover insurance, agriculture, investments, etc. need to have a federal agency covering them and each state must have a uniform set of rules that they can enforce. While it makes sense to have divisions in morality laws among the states, there is no need to have separate rules, regulations, fees, and other restrictions with commerce.

The policy of the American government is to leave their citizens free, neither restraining nor aiding them in their pursuits.

-Thomas Jefferson

Chapter 3:

Socialism's Plight

There is no form of modern government that compares to the perfection of socialistic communism. It provides for all citizens when they are in need. This includes those who have lost their job, are weakened by old age, become disabled, and those who are simply less gifted. A safety net is established for all citizens because all citizens will pay into the system at some point and take from it only in their time of need. It establishes a sense of national pride because you are not only working for yourself, but for your fellow man. There is no push to profit and the nature and drive of corporate greed are eliminated. The incentive to cheat is obsolete because you are in a utopian society with your fellow man. Ideas are shared and technology flourishes with everyone working as a team. The walls of competition are discarded. It almost sounds too good to be true.

A deeper look at a communist government approach reveals a couple of unavoidable truths. Socialism requires a strict adherence to certain rules (communism) or having a distinct advantage in resources. It must also be led by men or women who are completely selfless and who never put their own ambitions, pride, or welfare over that of the nation. The unfortunate reality of the socialist is that the government structure that is so endearing, is also very fragile. If a country fails to eliminate personal greed, falls victim to a bad leader, or does not have something to offer the rest of the world in a capitalistic format, then that country will always struggle and eventually crumble.

What rules are needed to make socialism successful and are they reasonable for the average American? This is a tough question given the vastly different backgrounds shared by the American people. I have my own thoughts on the issue, but you will have to develop your own thoughts as well and make your own decision. The key to any dilemma is to evaluate what it will take to make that choice successful and decide if you are willing to make the needed sacrifices.

Capitalism, conversely, feeds upon a person's more basic instincts of self-preservation and greed. This is not a flattering statement, but it is the foundation for a strong economic approach and it is extremely durable. Capitalism can outlast even the worst leaders (thank God) and poor legislation. Conversely, socialism is not quite as lucky and it is important to understand why.

Not all socialist countries appear to be in line to suffer the fate and slings that destroyed the Soviet Union. Some successes are fairly easy to understand and certainly make sense when examined on the surface. Venezuela, Bahrain, and Qatar are all extremely socialist even though they do have some elected officials or a more traditional monarchy. They all have an enviable spring of resources that have enabled them to build immense wealth, of which a portion is filtered down to its citizens. They do not suffer the common plight of the stereotypical socialist country. However, they do struggle with many of the human rights issues that are common to this type of government.

In Venezuela, it is not an uncommon practice to see political prisoners because of the harsh rule of an "elected" president. The leadership of this country has a history of firm rule and harsh responses to opposition. It wields a powerful display of strength over a large inventory of oil and the citizens of its nation. There are also reports of judges being executed for making "wrong" decisions in their trials as well and providing some of the worst prison conditions in the world. The corruption of the framework of this country has led to a poor distribution of wealth and declining quality of life throughout the land. With so many citizens falling into complete poverty, a rise in prostitution and the trafficking of people for both slavery and sexual exploitation has taken place. A country that prides itself in being a beacon for socialism and in protecting its dependent citizens, has evolved into a land of great wealth for a few as well as great poverty for most.

Bahrain and Qatar are both monarchies, but adhere to a socialist dynamic with their government operations. They are both very wealthy with their respective reserves of oil and natural gas. Many of the ideals that Americans would consider social injustices are masked under the cloak of the Nation of Islam. Limitation in regard to drinking alcohol, eating in public during Ramadan, and the inequality of women are direct results of their religion. It can be argued that they are not a product of socialism. Still, both countries struggle with many of the same human rights issues found in Venezuela. There are several practices that are common in both countries that would be challenging to accept in the United States.

The general inequality of women with regard to religion is the tip of the iceberg. Women are rarely protected against domestic abuse and marriage contracts are in strict favor of men. They also engage in various degrees of torture for those that are imprisoned for both political and criminal reasons. Discrimination is rampant. The heirarchy generally starts with different branches of native Muslims positioned on top of the pecking order and other religions, races, and nationalities fall well below them. Classes are created and outsiders are dehumanized. Human trafficking is common because of the promise of high wages in both countries. Furthermore, there have been many cases were hopeful workers have been trapped into servitude and/or sexual exploit. Bahrain has been labeled as one of the more progressive countries in the Middle East, but even with their efforts in women's suffrage, equality, and judicial fairness, it still struggles with its human rights.

It would be difficult to label any of these countries as successful even with their respective accumulations of wealth. By contrast, many have credited China as being an economic success because of its socialist foundation. China's structure is not complicated and could probably be duplicated in the United States. We would just need to decide if we are willing to accept the changes needed to make it work. China decided to take a communist approach because it identified itself as a developing country. Through their own research, they surmised that democratization could only follow modernization and could not precede it. If there is any consistent approach to life in the history of the Chinese people, it is an exacting approach to decision making. They also have a very different view of government than most Americans. Their approach is another way for them to organize themselves and their lives by providing a uniform discipline. China as a whole and the Chinese people feel that they are moving forward with their government blazing the trail.

China generally has strong leadership. The country evaluates its leaders based on their past successes and their perceived level of acumen for the job. There is a sense that, in their culture, maintaining harmony is important. Advancement is critical. A strong technology base and an effort to grow their knowledge is a never-ending quest. They have massive cities in terms of both population and structural growth. China has some amazing places and presents a combination of respectful preservation of its history and traditions along with extremely competitive growth and expansion. It is easy for many Americans to envy the positives of China because they are abundant and clear.

As mentioned earlier, socialism is delicate and it would not be fair to talk about the triumphs of China without also addressing the sacrifices that are being made to make it work. The first glaring weakness for the Chinese is the lack of a modern legal system. There are few laws in the country and judges are appointed by the state to make decisions that are not always backed by a written law or precedent. There is very little due process and a lot of discretion is given to the legal authority. This has opened the door to mass corruption and severe violations of many of the human rights that we find to be critical in this country. Your fate when faced with a court decision is clearly in the hands of the state and the resulting decision may have little to do with how right or wrong you may have been in your actions. This is further exemplified in the government's prosecution of citizens who speak out against its practices, monopolies, and even its religious movements. They have even gone so far as to block Internet sites that advocate and discuss different religions and government structures.

Many nations throughout the world felt that granting the summer Olympic Games to China would apply pressure to resolve many of the human rights issues found in such a modern nation. Yet, it actually led to some embarrassing accounts. Protesting was crushed during the games. Protesters were deported or they were detained and then deported when the games ended. There were also established areas that were sanctioned for protesters. One had only to apply for a permit. All of the applications were withdrawn, vetoed, or suspended. The government even went so far as to send some applicants to labor camps to reconsider their ideas about the Chinese authority. The workers for many of the new stadiums were rounded up and taken from the Olympic site because the government feared their poor appearance reflected negatively on China's image as a modern, thriving nation. The press had its difficulties as well. Interference was exercised through violence and intimidation and no Tibetan protest coverage was allowed.

Religious persecution in China should be of interest to Americans because of religion's relationship to the very formation of this country. China is governed only by atheists and although there have been confessed followers of various religions, they suffer discrimination and limitations to their political careers. However, the overall struggle is much deeper. All religions must be announced and registered with the state for approval. There are limitations as to the type of each religion that can be practiced as well as who its identified leaders can be. This has led to underground religions and worship. The Pope can only be recognized as the leader of the Catholic Church in this way.

China's treatment of the Tibetan monks is widely known. The Chinese government has disallowed the concept of reincarnation. When a leader was believed by his faith's followers to have been established in this manner, he was captured and held by the authorities. Tibetan monks now have several rules to follow in order to carry out their religious practices. They can have only a certain number of monks, must denounce the Dalai Lama as their leader, must memorize and recite certain loyalties to the Chinese government, and carry out other actions that are in direct conflict with their beliefs. Other various religions have suffered torture, forced labor, and imprisonment. It has been reported that the government has even targeted different religions for organ harvesting.

The human rights issues are more indirect when studying the potential shortcomings of socialism. The direct implications are more important when establishing exactly why a socialist structure of government is so delicate. Would Americans be willing to obey the practices of China in order to implement a more socialist structure? The belief of a more socialized

America hinges on this question. It is impossible to have the personal freedoms we enjoy today with an increasingly government-controlled economy if you do not have the resources to sell on a capitalistic stage. It has never worked both ways historically and there are no signs that it would work today.

The problem that must be addressed by any socialist country is making sure that the government can afford the healthcare, education, protection, and other needs of the people. Without controlling the work-flow, birth rates, and habits of the population, a government cannot be sure that it will be able to pay for its expenses. The people have to produce revenue and the expenses must be controlled. China understands this and has implemented strict regulations for their citizens on how they must work and where they must live. China is far from being the modern day Renaissance that they would like the world to believe.

In China, workers are divided into two groups. They have the urban group that has the more modern jobs and are considered to be the more sophisticated social class. They also have the rural jobs that are agriculture related. For the latter group to move to the former, they have to go through a stringent process that generally comes down to the contacts that person may or may not have in the government. If a person works outside of their allotted geographic area, then they lose their social benefits with no private alternative. That would mean no healthcare, food, housing, education, etc.

Rural workers are treated as second-class citizens and are the true laborers of China. They get second-rate schools, hospitals, and other socialized institutions.

Americans must realize that social programs must be accompanied by social restrictions. It cannot work both ways. The common denominator of any economy is the money that it takes to run it. A capitalistic society can limit the expenses of the government and change tax rates to make a system work. Socialist countries must depend on the work of the people to fund the nation's considerable costs. Too many weak links will cause that nation to crumble under its responsibilities to its people. Work-flow and movement must be orchestrated correctly because small movements and trends can disrupt the system. Spain has had considerable problems lately with older Europeans retiring in their country. With socialized medicine, they pay for everyone with only the tax dollars created in Spain. They cannot control the demographics in the country and are running a shortage of payers compared to the number of payees—similar to the problem Americans are facing with Social Security. Socialism by itself cannot work. It must be followed with a strict set of rules and therein lies the relative success of Communism.

I can understand Communism, but not Socialism.

    -Lajos Kossuth

Chapter 4:

Healthcare Is My Right

The latest battle cry for healthcare is to declare that it is everyone's right and that America is the last industrialized nation to adopt a universal healthcare system. The healthcare reformers have been demonstrative in their statements about the dissenters being baby killers, unfair to the less fortunate and religious hypocrites. Blame and finger pointing took center stage in a circus of debate and the real issues to healthcare reform took a back seat to the lions, acrobats, and clowns (mostly clowns). Still, behind the curtains is an excellent opportunity for economic fundamentals to drive a lasting solution that would work for everyone.

The first issue to cover is whether or not healthcare reform is important at all and if it is a subject that needs to be addressed. The answer is *yes*. You can clearly see that the topic is worth exploration because there is a poorly functioning market attached to it. The problem is that we have a government that is entirely too quick to take control of a need rather than to address its flaws. Of course, this gray area is the fuel for any debate between liberals and conservatives. If the free market cannot develop a system that is safe, reliable, affordable, and logistically possible, then it needs to be moved under Washington's watch along with roads and the military. From this perspective, the liberals have a point. The problem was never a priority for the conservatives and, for this reason, they share some responsibility for the social legislation that was adopted.

There is no definitive answer as to whether or not healthcare coverage can be adequately handled by the private sector. The key for a capitalist society is to try the free market approach first. Socialism should be the last resort. Road construction is an interesting example. This was another issue in which the government jumped into the pool head first without considering the private market. It makes logistical sense for the government to maintain roads because it may be difficult for landowners to coordinate their borders and maintain a reliable system. Regardless, due process was not applied and we will never know if a private approach would have worked. We voluntarily skipped into consistently poor road conditions, potholes, inefficient workers, poor traffic flow, and other conditions that are typical of a socialized service.

What would be the worst thing that could happen if roads were controlled through a private market? You would certainly see some changes. Borders would have to be leveled and landowners would have to work together to make the system work. You would probably see more toll booths to collect for the private owners. Collaboration would have to take place for this as well so that you would not stop every few miles to drop in your change. This does not sound like an overwhelming argument to privatize roads, but we need to consider the positives. You would have a market deciding where roads are needed and how big they should be. Drivers would have to pay for their usage on a more individual basis and so cruising and Sunday drives would be limited. Carpooling would now make more financial as well as environmental sense.

I believe that technology would evolve to adopt some kind of screening system that just counts your car as it goes by a sensor and then bills the driver at the end of the month. There are many toll roads that already use this kind of system. Poorly maintained roads and less needed roads would die off as better and more demanded roads are built (and as need and competition dictate). Taxes would be reduced. This might not work; it would certainly be a mighty upheaval at this point to try. The point of this example is that when you have the opportunity to choose private or public, try private first and then go with public if it fails. We had this opportunity with healthcare reform and did not take advantage of it. Still, that is not going to stop me from analyzing the possibilities of a private reform.

Affordability is the major concern with healthcare. Can the private market system correct this problem or is the expense just high and unaffordable because of the nature of healthcare? I believe that both issues can be addressed and corrected. We will approach this issue just as someone would try to lose weight—with diet and exercise. It is tough to just focus on one area that needs improvement as a way to solve the overall problem. To fix healthcare, the costs need to be lowered and the private market system needs to be corrected. This would be an appropriate time to state another key focus of government intervention. It does have its place. The government should serve the economy and protect the people. Military, fire, and police all serve the protection role, but many forget about the government's power to conduct the free market properly and promote competition. Regulating healthcare insurance and promoting competition has been a failure to this point.

The first point to examine is who exactly has the authority to regulate the industry. According the McCarran-Ferguson Act, states regulate all insurance. It is not viewed as interstate commerce and is not subject to the Sherman Anti-Trust Act, Clayton Act, or any other anti-trust legislation. This is a problem for a number of different reasons. The first issue is limiting insurance providers to conducting business within its company's state borders. As a broker, I have literally had clients travel hundreds of miles (or met them half-way) to sign annuity documents because no insurance products can be sold across state lines. This is a crippling blow to the industry's ability to provide competitive choices. There is no need for an industry to operate under such constraints. It limits choices and promotes monopolies. In general, monopolies are not a big deal. They either operate efficiently or other firms will take notice of their poor management and gross profits. That is when a competitor emerges. Monopolies only become an issue when they pressure an overgrown government into bending the rules for them.

This brings us to out next problem—high barriers to entry into the health insurance industry. Health insurance providers have enjoyed massive profits only because they are able to control and sustain an inefficient monopoly. If the market were open, then you would see a flood of new providers who are eager to take a cut of this massive pie. Why is it such a challenge to enter the industry? We have already discussed the state regulations and there are certain hurdles to be jumped to just get passed them. However, the larger problem comes with the provider networks. This is an intricate web that must be woven in today's environment. It is a ridiculous arrangement that seems to only exist for the purpose of keeping monopolies in business. Premiums continue to rise, profits continue to rise, new entrants are few, and merger after merger pushes the healthcare insurance industry into worse conditions for the consumer.

It is time to modernize insurance. To correct any economic problem, a free market approach must be attempted before nationalization takes place. The healthcare industry is no different. There are stories of doctors getting in legal trouble because they offer unlimited services on retainer for a monthly fee. In a free market, there would be no problem with this approach and competition would immediately spark. However, this is not allowed because it is forbidden to be an insurer and a doctor at the same time. The system must be obeyed because it is the system. It does nothing to promote safety for the patients and it certainly does not exist to keep prices in an affordable range. It is an obsolete set of rules that only exists to keep those in power, in power.

Our first step is to regulate healthcare on a national level. Every doctor must register their services with a national clearing firm. This will keep track of any black marks on their record as well as provide information about the doctor to insurance providers. This is similar to the U-4 tracking done for investment advisors.

Once the proper degrees and steps are taken to achieve the title of doctor, free market business comes into play. You start with a clean slate and maintaining that clean slate allows you to continue to practice. You can conduct your business in any way that you see fit, but know that all customer complaints are recorded and available to the public. Of course, this could become obsolete as well. I am basically describing exactly what Yelp does for the restaurant industry. It is not a big stretch to think this is feasible for healthcare. Also, insurance providers do not get to choose which doctors you can and cannot see. The choice is yours as long as their credentials are in order and they are properly registered.

Coverage should be able to cross state lines. Heath insurance providers should be able to set up shop in any location they want and they can choose the coverage that they would like to offer. Plans that fall short or do not cover what is needed by the public will be replaced in a competitive free market as there will be money to be made because of the oversight. Opening this door to competition will bring prices down for a number of reasons. First, insurance companies will have their profits cut and will have to be more efficient with their business operations. Massive profits will no longer be aligned with massive waste. Secondly, as healthcare insurance becomes more affordable, more people will pay into the plans and this will bring down the cost per person. Dropping state-by-state oversight, monitoring monopolistic behavior more aggressively, and tearing down the barriers of entry to this industry will do more for healthcare than anything imaginable in the social spectrum.

With my solution of taking healthcare to a freer system, I believe that most issues of the Right are addressed. The major fears of this side for a nationalized system are tax increases, lines, losing more complicated procedures and tests, losing skilled doctors, and prioritization of care. Keeping healthcare out of the government's hands is the key element to eliminating these concerns. Nonetheless, the Left does have valid arguments that need an audience as well. How do we care for the poor, the elderly, illegal aliens, young adults coming off of their parent's coverage, and others that are currently uninsured? Is there a level of commitment and taxes that should be expected from this set of people before they are allowed medical coverage? How are pre-existing conditions handled? These are all tough questions and they certainly lead to an infinite supply of answers.

All kinds of numbers were thrown around in the healthcare debate of the 2008 and 2012 elections about how many Americans are currently without coverage. The Left displayed numbers as high as 60 million people. The Right countered by saying that number should be closer to 10 million people after you factor out citizens that can afford coverage and choose not to have it as well as illegal aliens. Like most things, the truth probably lies somewhere in the middle. So, how do we cover everyone in a way that is affordable for the nation? That is a tough question and one that may not be answerable or possible. Still, the United States strives to provide its citizens with the opportunity for a healthy, happy life. It does not mandate that it should take on the burden of providing for all of its citizens when they are in need. This is a harsh reality that we need to understand before moving forward. We have examined the necessary side of socialized programs and without the strict provision of workers supplying a system; we cannot depend on it for care. America needs to make sure that any government assistance provided keeps incentives in line with human condition so that it is not subject to be taken advantage of and wasted.

The elderly and the disabled are currently covered under Medicaid. Workers pay their FICA taxes and this practice funds the healthcare of these two groups. The disabled of our nation have no say in their plight and should be covered. Also, it is difficult to argue against the elderly getting coverage because they have paid into the current system their entire lives. Furthermore, as the baby boomers age and move past age 65, they will be eligible for benefits and it will be expensive. The current workers of the United States will be expected to cover these costs and they could rise to 30% or more of the nation's total GDP. Like most socialized systems, Medicare does have problems. It is abused by both the providers and the recipients. There are bogus and excessive claims as well as bogus and excessive charges. This is the problem posed by any system that takes away the incentive for people to ration and make efficient decisions.

What do we do? The system is in place and we cannot deny the elderly a plan that was designed for their twilight years, especially after they paid into it for 10, 20, 30, or maybe 40 years. It is not their fault that the money was wasted and that the system is bankrupt. The solution does not come from immediately denying all benefits, but from overhauling the system. Anyone that is disabled is covered. Accidents do happen and only people that are responsible enough to cover themselves with a disability policy will have anything near the quality of life they are accustomed to prior to being disabled. This is a tough system to be abused because no one will disable themselves to receive meager benefits.

The real issue is dealing with retirement and Medicare for the elderly. Medicare is a complete mess because it is being funded through tax dollars, but still charges premiums to some of its recipients. It is completely inefficient and wasteful and it needs to go. Social Security is also a monstrous waste of money and it needs to go. All citizens that have paid into the system and are 50 years of age or older should get the benefits they've accrued. From that age and younger, all benefits are eliminated and everyone under 50 is sent a check returning what they have already paid into the system.   They will be responsible for their own healthcare now and during their retirement years.

This is far from a perfect system because you still run the risk of people not saving or protecting themselves and falling into the hands of tax dollar support. After all, a hospital cannot turn away a patient. So, I suggest a compromise. All Social Security money and taxes are returned to the younger age group in the form of an HSA. Health Savings Accounts are a great way to save without wasting money on insurance premiums. You are given a high deductible plan that you may not use when you are young, but will certainly use when you are older. You choose the plan and the provider, and the dollars that were wasted on government programs are now deposited into an account that is set aside for your personal healthcare and your retirement. Contributions are tax deductible and reasonable expenses come out of the account tax-free. Early withdrawals are taxed and penalized and these funds are deposited into an account that will cover the uninsured and others that do not pay for their medical needs.

A system like this would have several results. There would be a feeding frenzy over all of the new clients that are shifted from government insurance to private providers. Coverage would get amazingly competitive and rates would fall. Everyone would have the opportunity to be covered and health insurance would be affordable. The initial tax bill for this plan would be expensive, but in the long run it will save the American people trillions of dollars. We are long overdue for a system that aligns need and personal responsibility when it comes to healthcare. HSAs are the future of healthcare and if the government truly wants to support healthcare coverage for all citizens, then they will not try to find a way to make Health Savings Accounts a government controlled tax producer.

Another reform that needs to be created for healthcare is to adopt a new format. Clearly, if your health is evaluated on an annual basis, you will pay more in premiums as you age. This needs to be corrected. The best way to do this would be to apply an approach to healthcare coverage that is similar to life insurance. Your coverage should work in conjunction with your HSA. You choose when you would like to start your coverage and you are evaluated by a doctor of the insurance provider. They determine what your annual rate will be and it is set for the life of your term coverage. If you agree with the provider to pay less now and more later, then that is fine. The point is that you are covered for a set number of years at a pre-determined premium. It cannot go up if you acquire a new illness along the way. You have until the age of 30 to get covered and can be listed under your parents' plan until that age. Of course, a 21 year old would get a less expensive annual premium than a 30 year old. I actually believe that this transformation would be an evolutionary result of our new free market.

Everyone else that is not covered will fall into two categories— citizens and non-citizens. Citizens will receive medical care just as we have always provided it. The hospital provides the services needed and reports the loss on taxes. Some subsidies would be available from the government and that would be funded by the penalties assessed when early withdrawals are made from HSA accounts. The services will be adequate, but nothing like the care of a private hospital. Of course, that would be no different from today's situation. It will make sense for all citizens who can work to go ahead and work. The Laffer Curve should be nicely illustrated by our new incentive to work and keep more of what is earned. Basic care will always be in place, but it is imperative that we remove the incentive to not work for those that are able-bodied.

Illegal aliens are a different story altogether. Providing healthcare to a non-citizen of the country should be the discretion of the hospital, but they should clearly display their policies on the matter.   The government will provide assistance, but not financial assistance. A non-citizen must state their nation of origin in a participating hospital before they are treated so that country can be billed at a later time. At the end of the year, the US government will start compiling all of the costs of healthcare provided to citizens through normal tax reporting. A bill will be issued to each country listed and it will either be paid in full or not. The proceeds of the collection of this bill will be distributed to the participating hospitals and it may or may not cover their costs. A hospital may change its participation standing each year and they can base it on repayment from the responsible country.

Controlling healthcare costs is also important in solving the affordability crisis. There must be an incentive for the public to only use the system when they are in need. We must also relay the costs of care to the individual so that they can shop for alternatives and the market can work properly to regulate costs. The HAS program would be a major step in eliminating $20 tongue depressors as well as operations and other procedures that push costs in the thousands-of-dollars arena. The patient needs to be aware of all of the ingredients needed to treat their condition so that they can choose the mix of products that they would like to use to get there. Prescription drugs are moving this direction and people can choose the pharmacy they would like to use as well as any generic alternatives that may be available.

My stepfather worked for an organization called Project Cure whose purpose was to go to other nations to evaluate their medical needs and assist them with supplies. He was once in the Ukraine talking to a man that had his knee replaced and asked him to explain the procedure. The man bragged about how wonderful his doctor is and how pleased he was with his brand new knee. Now, medical procedures like a knee replacement are not common in many parts of the world and this man's story is no exception. He explained that he found the doctor that could do the procedure, but had to procure the replacement knee on his own. It ended up being a black market transaction and was quite an accomplishment in its own right. Many countries also make patients provide the gloves and other items needed by the doctor to perform the procedure. I am not advocating that patients arrive to the doctor's office with a handful of equipment and parts needed for every visit. Yet, they do need to be connected to the individual costs. This can only happen through patients being billed and given an itemized list of everything they are charged by the hospital. A system that has a $15 co-pay which allows infinite expenses is inefficient and extremely wasteful. With any demand, supply will follow. Medical supplies would be available to the public for purchase and these items would be rated, reviewed, and affordably priced.

Tort reform has had a long-standing relationship with healthcare. Many studies have shown that lawsuits are diminishing from their peak, but the threat still causes a huge expense for the healthcare industry. Even if a hospital is not sued, they still must cover themselves in the event that they do fall prey to the *big one*. Insurance premiums are a massive expense of drug companies, doctors, and hospitals and they must be kept in check.

We cannot eliminate a person's ability to sue when they have a legitimate claim, but we must examine what a fair payout would be and whether there is a reasonable risk involved with the drug or procedure the patient is undertaking. If it is clear no other alternative is available or that the client chose the riskier course, then no damages should be awarded. Drug companies already have to have FDA approval to release drugs to the public. If drugs are later found to be a detriment, then the government is to blame for poor oversight and the individual firm will suffer the damage to their reputation. Only medical providers that blatantly abuse a client through improper care should pay settlements. Multi-million dollar awards have been out of hand for a long time and are obnoxiously overstated. Most people will not make anywhere near this amount of money in their lifetimes and their pain and suffering is not more important than the entire healthcare industry. Reasonable settlements are another component to controlling costs and our nation has to understand that there is an element of risk associated with any medical procedure.

Realigning the public mindset with the costs of medical treatments, along with opening the underlying markets for supplies and medications is the key to a successful free healthcare market. It is also a reasonable transition for our current system. The United States cannot support socialized healthcare. We are already behind on Medicare and Social Security and the debt is increasing every year. We live in a country of opportunity, not entitlement. There are many countries all over the world that find our situations humorous. If someone is unable to provide for himself (or herself) here, then he would never make it in many other countries.

The only thing our government should do is provide a competitive market place that creates the best healthcare in the world. It is available to anyone that wants to work for it and it is affordable because of market dictated pricing. Without taking strict social measures in regard to working, controlling where people can live, and reducing benefits, socialized medicine will forever be a cancer feeding upon the American economy. If we can open up the system, you may find it evolving into a more streamlined and customized source of coverage. While one person's coverage may offer the occasional massage, another's might offer assistance with a gym membership fee. You would find premium rebates for people that keep their weight at a normal level or display other healthy living habits. You could take the option to see a chiropractor, physical therapist, get a massage, acupuncture, or maybe even discounts for athletic related companies like Dick's or REI. The possibilities are endless with a free market. Growing the market is the most important element in correcting our healthcare dilemma and it will open doors to services that have never previously been available.

The right way to reign in healthcare costs is not by applying more government, and more controls, and making it more like the post office. It's by making it more like a consumer driven market.

    -Mitt Romney

Chapter 5:

Banking and Bailouts

Most free market economists are against government bailouts and I am no exception. I believe that the market closes doors that need to be closed. Sometimes this can be the result of an obsolete product or because of a poorly operating business model. There are also plenty of arguments illustrating that a small amount of unemployment is always going to be present in our economy because it is an indicator of growth. Students are graduating and business is evolving.

When the government interferes with the free market, it can have devastating results. Most companies suffer or go out of business for a very tangible reason. Supporting a company that is no longer competitive is both wasteful and delaying progress. Examining a few situations that involve government intervention is important because it has a contrasting result from the free market solution.

The first market I would like to consider is the auto industry. The United States government (taxpayers) has spent billions of dollars to keep several companies from going under and filing bankruptcy. Arguably, the intentions were good because funding these companies has helped many Americans keep their jobs. However, after looking at the facts, this expense has become difficult to rationalize to the people actually supplying the funding. Spending taxpayer dollars without their actual consent is becoming a far too common occurrence. Let us look at the industry and try to decide if supporting it was a good investment for the citizens of this country.

In 2009 the U.S. pledged $25 billion to the big three automakers in Detroit and most of that allotment was targeted at employee benefits and healthcare. The refusal of the government to let these companies go under is also a refusal to address their issues. The clear culprit of the auto industry is the unionization of its employees. Many of the jobs held in this arena are low skilled, manual labor professions. I will not deny that the workers are good at their craft or even that they put long, strenuous hours. Still, a lot of businesses have employees like this, but they are not paid a premium amount that is detrimental to that company's very existence. The unions are so entrenched in Detroit automobile manufacturing that car manufacturers are not even opening new plants in the Mecca of car production. When you have a system that pays its employees regardless of their performance, company profitability, or even seasonal changes, then you have a big problem.

The free market and government intervention are clearly at work in this case and the contrast of the two sets up an interesting study. The government bailout feels like we are simply throwing money away to support a clearly failing system. The Detroit auto industry has already proven that it cannot manage its employees to make a competitive product with an affordable business model. Several of these companies are actually losing money for every car that they sell. The fact that they are even in business is a miracle of any economy. Manual laborers are demanding high pay, great benefits, unbelievable pensions, and other perks that they do not deserve. They do not deserve these things because they are not profitable enough to warrant them. This is not a judgment call, but a clear statement issued by the free market and the profitability of the very companies that employ them. The tax funding of these companies is a waste and something that the American taxpayer will have to eat as a loss.

The market response is much more encouraging. A different portion of the country actually has legislation in place that promotes the free market and competition and it comes in the form of "right to work" laws. This legislation correctly aligns the market with employment for several reasons. First, it gives anyone the "right to work" regardless of their union involvement. Prospective employees do not have to pass a prerequisite union membership in order to gain eligibility to be hired. They do not have to pay union dues or follow any other bureaucratic procedures. Next, employees are hired, paid, and kept (or fired) on their credentials and performance. When competition is present, a wrongfully terminated worker will gladly be acquired by a rival firm because of their level of productivity. Racism, sexism, and all other forms of discrimination put firms at a severe disadvantage as their competition is now enabled to cherry pick the best performers. Forced unionization is another form of socialism and it has demolished the American auto industry.

The market format of the "right to work" states has been incredibly successful in these areas. They provide great jobs that are consistent and secure because they coexist with the success of the firms that provide them. For this reason, there have been factories popping up all over the place in the states that do not allow unions to dictate hiring practices. Mississippi, Alabama, Tennessee, and others have been recipients of foreign companies moving into their towns and have been injected with a nice economic boom. This is a wonderful illustration of the positive power of the free market as opposed to the anchor that any socialist program inflicts on its recipient. In addition to the union rules offered by these states, they also have the benefit of lower taxes on employees and corporations. This is another sizable advantage over the traditional manufacturing states in the automotive industry.

You would assume that I am also very much against the bailouts received by the financial services industry and you are partially correct. The banks and other institutions that received money from the taxpayer have a little bit more of a legitimate claim than the auto industry. They were the unlucky targets of a number of socialized programs that were aimed at making housing affordable for every American. It is a wonderful concept and I would agree that the intentions were good. However, just like many other manipulations by the government, it had negative side effects. In this instance the results were devastating.

The Fair Housing and the Community Reinvestment Acts were reenergized during the 90's in an effort to make home ownership available to every American. Banks receiving FDIC coverage were required to show significant increases in loans to higher risk, lower income, and minority applicants. There were a couple of critical changes made to the lending markets because of this legislation. The first change was that people who were previously unable to gain approval for a loan were now being approved. The second change was that borrowers were also now able to get approval for a higher loan than they could under the previous conditions set by credit score, debt, equity, and income. So, the country saw a huge change in the housing market. People were now able to get their first home and other applicants were getting approval for even bigger houses.

Naturally, banks and other lenders were concerned with this practice because it would undoubtedly mean that their risk would go up and that defaults would increase. So, the government made the lenders a deal. They told them that standards would also be dropped for Fannie Mae and Freddie Mac loans so that lenders could initiate the loan and then pass it along to these indirectly backed government agencies. This was a win-win for banks because they were now able to loan to just about anyone and defer all of their risk to these companies that had vowed to purchase any mortgage from them. You can see the conflict of interest arising from a situation like this and the ultimate failure resulting from a hybrid system developed in a free market with socialist regulations.

The results were disastrous. The free market system drove banks to approve everyone they possibly could. It is a system that operates on profit being the key indicator for a business practice being a success. Loan numbers were up and business was booming. The socialized side removed all onuses from the gatekeepers and that is a critical disconnect when this is the group deciding for or against making a loan. When faced with possible fines for not lending as well as the safety net of government backing, all loans became reasonable to America's lending institutions.

When the consequences of lowered lending standards were realized, there were only a few options available to all parties involved. Of course, cover-up and government manipulation was the easiest route to take. In 2003 and 2004, the first major errors surfaced for Fannie Mae and Freddie Mac. Freddie Mac admitted to overstating profits by $5 billion. Fannie Mae had a large number of accounting errors that led to costs in excess of $6 billion to correct them. Both firms have also been charged with illegal campaign contributions and other data manipulation used to maximize leadership bonuses and government subsidies. There were even government officials covering up the blatant problems of these institutions in an effort to keep them conducting their day-to-day business. With a great deal at stake, it was imperative that these entities remain solvent and off the radar.

By comparison, in a free market system, this type of crisis is formidable. Yet, it is also manageable. The parties in charge of accounting errors are fined or possibly imprisoned and competitors swoop in to buy the assets from the failing company. The difference in this situation comes from the high level of government intervention. Our officials in Washington were just as entrenched in the success of Freddie Mac and Fannie Mae as any board member of the actual company. They had financial and political incentives to keep problems away from the press and continue funding. It is extremely difficult to admit it was a mistake to give low-income families a means to home ownership. It is unbearable to admit that the lending practices developed over a hundred years of trial and error in the free market were actually correct and needed no tweaking from the U.S. Government. This arrangement and relationship is not completely incomparable to the relationship Arthur Anderson had with Enron. They knew that Enron collapsing would make a huge dent in Arthur Anderson's long-term viability. It made sense to cook the books.

It is with a heavy heart that I agree with the bailout of financial institutions. Banks and other lenders do share responsibility in the mayhem of the housing crisis and they have paid for that with tumbling stock prices and several companies declaring bankruptcy. In a perfect world, they would have stood up to the original legislation in place and simply paid the fines in the short run, trusting that the market would one day prove them to be correct in the matter. Still, this is an incredibly risky decision. When the government is holding the cards and laying out a path that you are requested to follow, you almost have to take it. The government has established itself as the safety net for our financial sector through FDIC insurance. They set the regulations for deposit ratios, interest rates, and disclosures. Financial institutions understand the ramifications of defying Washington's will. When the entity that makes the rules asks you to do something, it is generally in your best interest to acquiesce. This is another burden of a large government. It makes it easy to put legislation in place and then blame its failure on the private entities that were expected to make it work.

It's not by augmenting the capital of the country, but by rendering a greater part of that capital active and productive than would otherwise be so, that the most judicious operations of banking can increase the industry of the country.

-Adam Smith

Chapter 6:

Educate the Children

Children are a difficult topic when it comes to evaluating a free market approach and finding an economically sound format for their development. They need to be monitored and guided as they develop physically and mentally into adulthood. There are many questions to answer when it comes to education and children. Do the smarter kids need to be separated from the ones that are falling behind? Should some students get free meals, special assistance, or lower standards? Are grading and standardized tests biased or unfair? Do music, sports, clubs, and other extracurricular activities have their place in school? Should classes for non-English speakers, affirmative action, and child daycare exist?

It seems to be most appropriate to apply socialist systems to our children because they require a roadmap and direction to properly develop. Still, like most socialist programs, these expenditures need to be tightly monitored and carefully executed. It is important to evaluate children to find out exactly what needs they may have because of the vastly different backgrounds that produce them.

Even the most adamant supporter of nature in the nature v. nurture argument would agree that a child from a good home has a significant advantage over a child from a broken or abusive one. There are kids out there that are clearly more talented in math, science, music, or any other given discipline. Without the guidance and structure in place to cultivate these talents, they could be wasted. Combining natural talent with a strong home life provides the best odds for a successful individual. What if you had to choose one of these scenarios over the other one? Would you want to be richly talented, but come from a poor home that may potentially prevent you from properly developing? Or, would you want to be average in every way, but come from a supportive home that provides advice and a strong foundation throughout your life?

I think I would personally have to go with the latter. Having a great support system is critical for a child and young adult to properly mature. A strong work ethic and proper understanding of personal finance (two skills that are generally developed in the home) can still be an effective route in becoming a successful person.

So, what does this have to do with education? Well, the key to growing a solid future with our children lies in developing a culture of strong foundations in the home. It seems that a lot of issues develop from a substandard domestic environment for children. They are raised by adults (or minors) who were not given the tools needed to succeed in life. Some of these children are able to do it on their own or they have a talent that overcomes their environment. However, most children follow a similar road as their parents and they have children that are doomed to the same fate. It is a cyclical problem and it grows each year as more children are conceived in situations like this. You see responsible adults generally having fewer children because they only have so much time and money to properly raise them.

This gives us two items that must be addressed. How do we deal with the children that are born into less than ideal situations and how do we improve this situation? I do not think that most people would blame a child for poor performance in school or even behavioral problems when they come from an abusive or neglectful home. These children were given a raw deal and are simply a product of their environments. They do need some help and I believe that tax dollars should be allocated for their benefit. This may seem contrary to my government laissez faire comments from earlier, but they are really very complimentary.

As long as incentives stay in line with social programs, they can be beneficial and affordable. We need to develop our rights in the United States as a type of currency. Every citizen should be required to give a little in support of their country, especially when their country is supporting them. So, how does someone on welfare contribute? They may not have the financial means to pay for their children or even for their own home, but they do have rights that can be used in exchange.

The right to vote and the right to have children can be exchanged for government assistance.   The right to vote is the easiest to argue because it also prevents politicians from paying for votes. Increases in welfare will be determined by citizens not on welfare. After all, they are the ones ultimately paying for it. Many citizens can empathize with someone going through a tough time and needing some assistance. The important thing to realize is that assistance should be a temporary fix until that person is able to get back on their feet and, once again, become a contributing citizen of this country. Our history is filled with people who died for the right to vote. It is not unreasonable to expect someone to support themselves for that same right.

Having a child takes two partners and raising a child properly also requires the contribution of two partners. Many times, a woman will have a baby with a man and that is the final joint contribution made in the life of that child. As much as I would like to mandate that fathers and mothers both take a proactive approach to raising their children, I believe that is unrealistic. However, holding them accountable for their actions is critical and possible.

If parents require welfare, then that need will cost them (both partners) the right to vote. They will also be limited to one child for benefits. The days of accumulating more and more children by unfit parents to maximize their government benefits needs to end. It would also make financial sense for tax payers to offer free vasectomies and tube tying procedures to anyone that has had that first child and receives welfare. It is an option that would take away the excuse of accidentally having another child to go on welfare in the future. In the long run, it will lift a huge financial burden on the workforce as well as prevent the frequency of births into unfit homes.

This may sound like a severe answer to this problem, but it is a fair one. Society should not have to helplessly stand by and continue cutting checks to people who are irresponsibly having children. The number of children that are abused, neglected, and put up for adoption would fall and the price of these procedures would be far less than the continued financing of our current situation. It would also hold fathers just as accountable as mothers. It would be a choice and it would be a step toward protecting children from incapable parents as well as growing the number of children that come from a firm foundation.

Conversely, I see no other affordable alternatives for our current trend other than more government control when it comes to human rights--communism. It is extremely expensive to apply socialist programs to a free market and free will society. It leaves the door open to abuse and influences decisions in a negative manner. If a person can own a home, cell phone, be fed, clothed, and have their healthcare taken care of without working, then they may choose that easier path in life. If a person is paid for each child that they have, then they may have multiple children.

Disconnecting a person's choices from the consequences of those choices is dangerous and a cancer upon any tax-paying society. While I genuinely dislike the idea of sterilizing anyone, we must limit the amount of money that is available for each child born into welfare. That is a dangerous incentive and creates an alarming demographic change as the non-working class out-breeds the taxpayers of this country. You may recall a previous statement about socialism only being viable if you have the money to pay for it. If you do not, drastic communist measures are the only alternative. I'd prefer to lose the socialist program over adopting communism or social engineering. This is a challenging problem and the only real solution is for individuals to take responsibility for their actions and lives. If that cannot be achieved, then coupling socialism with communism becomes one of the few workable solutions for this problem.

With that said, even the most capitalistic society is still going to be accountable for educating its children and some of that burden will fall on the taxpayer. Once again, the key to this situation is aligning services with incentives and consequences. This can be a tricky task when it comes to education. I believe that keeping our current amount of funding level for education can accomplish a lot if only a few adjustments are made. It is important to identify why schools are struggling, why quality teachers are difficult to find and maintain, and why education expenses inflate at a higher annual rate than most other goods and services. With the right changes, students could be better educated and good teachers would be rewarded for being more effective.

There have been many proposals to improve public schools and we need to address them. One of the most popular ideas is a system of using vouchers to reward schools that consistently produce good students with high test scores. Vouchers would allow a parent to send their child to any school that they choose. They could be used to identify good schools with quality educators and leadership. These schools would flourish and the unpopular schools would suffer. The idea is to promote competition and force the underperforming schools to step up and put forth a better product. The idea is a good one from an incentive standpoint, but I do not think that it will work in the long run. Private schools would be a sticky situation because even though government vouchers may be accepted, these institutions can still pick and choose the students that they would like to admit. This could lead to a big clash between private schools and the U.S. government. Also, schools need to become a cornerstone of the community. Busing students across town to a better school would be detrimental to that community's development. I like the thought behind the voucher system, but it is an incomplete solution in its current form.

"We should pay teachers more money." The idea is that if teachers received a better salary, then there would be more competition and the result would be better educators. This is not a bad thought, but we have to find a way to produce the money to pay teachers more. I believe that this can happen. If an idea is sound and worthwhile, then the budget needs to be adjusted to facilitate the change. Good ideas take sacrifice; not from the taxpayer, but by cutting expenses that do not climb as high on the list of priorities. It will be critical to start identifying waste in the education system if we ever want the ability to afford better teachers.

"Everyone should continue their education through the college level. If we can create our current level of production with a huge segment of the population having only a high school diploma, just think about what we could accomplish if these same people carried a college education." This is another thought that sounds great on the surface, but does not quite work in reality. College should be a way to divide the population. It should set apart the people that work harder or are more gifted. This sounds harsh, but it provides a means of evaluation and reestablishes the importance of high school. If everyone is pushed through to college, then graduating from high school becomes less meaningful. Graduating from high school needs to be an accomplishment in itself and it needs to signify that the graduate now has the tools to function in society. Improving the high school system is vital to this country and needs to become more momentous.

High schools need to be returned to their role as a fundamental institution within the community and provide an acceptable degree for potential employers. College should be used to refine skills for students that choose a particular career path that requires further development. A high school diploma should indicate that the graduate is a capable person with the drive and focus to consider being hired. It should not just be a piece of paper that is given to everyone simply because they are 18 years old and have been in high school for 4 years. So, the task is to make this level of schooling worthwhile as well as affordable to the taxpayer.

Social programs must be carefully implemented within the school system. If the government is going to fund education, then the money must not be wasted. I believe that music, athletics, and most other school programs are reasonable expenses. They do a great job of identifying talent in different areas early and encourage children to pursue what they do well and develop that skill. Children may not know where their talents lie until they are exposed to some of these different disciplines in school. We are able to establish foundations for children at an early age when they are able to identify their talents.

The more difficult decision arises when choosing to supply certain services to some children while they are not provided to others. Some children are slower learners than others and demand more of the teacher's time to digest the presented material. Many students receive only one wholesome meal each day and it comes from their school lunch. We also have translating services for non-English speakers as well as tutoring sessions. Some schools have daycares, special education programs, and after-school care. These programs can be quite expensive and so it is important to maintain them carefully. This would be another example where a taxpayer would earn the right to vote and those on public assistance would forfeit this right. If a parent is struggling to take care of his or her child, then a substantial meal (hopefully a healthy one) and care for the child after school (most end by midafternoon) can be a great help. It gives that parent the opportunity to get back on his or her feet without the child suffering. This system also disallows politicians buying votes and limits free-riding abuse. Taxpayers should have more say in how tax dollars are spent than those on public assistance at home or in the classroom.

Furthermore, these decisions need to be made at the state level. The state is responsible for balancing the budget and running the school systems. They have to decide if they would like to use the lottery system to provide additional funding or if they would like to run fewer social programs (or maybe pay their teachers less). The states should also edit their own curriculum. If one state wants to teach creationism and another wants to teach evolution, then that should be their choice. Neither theory of the universe's development lacks an element of faith from its believers. Each state needs to be held responsible for balancing its budget and making moral decisions about what is actually taught in school. Education can come a long way simply by aligning its direction with the proper decision makers.

The education system also needs to use its teachers more effectively. Teachers are employees of the state and should look for jobs openings based on where they would like to live. Yet, they should not expect to work at the same school every year. Teachers should be rotated from school to school throughout that metropolitan district. The principals and other leaders of each school will be held accountable for the performance of the students. If a particular school is struggling, then the leadership needs to be addressed. If the principals from the schools of that district find particular teachers to be the problem, then that issue too must be confronted. There are too many bad teachers and leaders in the school systems of this country. Both groups need to be evaluated, praised when appropriate, and fired when needed.

The key to a proper education funded through a sound economic foundation comes down to proper planning and aligning incentives correctly. Individuals must pay for the services that they receive in some way. Human beings find it very easy to get lazy and fall into the trap of giving up and letting the government supply their well-being. This is incredibly dangerous for them as they mature as well as expensive for the taxpayer. Children do need to be cared for and are deserving of assistance. They are our future and do not have a say in what kind of home life they will have. Some are very lucky and others fall into extremely unfortunate circumstances. Using a fundamental economic approach to educating our population is critical. It will produce better teachers, smaller classrooms, a better curriculum, proper decision making when it comes to religion, and a realistic approach to social services and taxing.

It was my teacher's genius, her quick sympathy, her loving tact which made the first years of my education so beautiful. It was because she seized the right moment to impart knowledge that made it so pleasant and acceptable to me.

    -Helen Keller

Chapter 7:

Give Me Your Poor, Your Tired, Your Huddled Masses

As the son of a Hungarian immigrant, I can empathize with anyone who wishes to come to the United States. My grandparents were victims of the Soviet assault on Eastern Europe. The communist system led to a clash between my grandfather's wine business and the competition from the state. My grandfather paid a premium price to the local grape growers to create a better product. This victory of capitalism had to be crushed, thus the financial success that resulted from triumphing over the state was short lived. My grandfather was imprisoned on a trumped-up charge of embezzlement.

After five months, my grandmother was able to locate the prison where he was being held—information that was not shared with her when the police knocked at the door to take him away. She then convinced the guards to allow her to wash his clothes. This provided him with a secret means of communication. My grandfather would prick his finger on a nail and write messages in blood to his wife. They were hidden in his socks among his dirty laundry. After nine months, he was given an ultimatum. He could confess in court and be freed or take a beating and remain in prison. He took the first option.

My grandfather put a couple of child seats on a bicycle that left the town of Gyor. They used back alleyways to avoid authorities and arousing suspicion. After eventually arriving at a taxi stand, they left for a bus station in the town of Mosonmaygarovar. The bus took my aunt, grandmother, and father to the border of Austria while my grandfather trailed them by motorcycle. After arriving at the border, they met with a smuggler. My grandfather paid him with his coat, a pair of shoes, and his motorcycle. They all loaded into a horse-drawn carriage lined with straw. After spending a few nights in an Austrian schoolhouse, they were on their way to America.

This was just the first part of their journey to becoming U.S. citizens. They acquired their green cards through an offer of asylum and proceeded to ready themselves for necessary testing. They learned English. This is not only a necessary tool to navigate the citizenship test, but essential for conducting business in the United States. Both of my grandparents worked very hard upon their arrival to build new lives for their family. My aunt holds multiple master's degrees. My father joined the Navy and later got his college degree in mechanical engineering. My Hungarian family went through the proper channels of citizenship and is a testament to the land of opportunity. Citizenship is not an easy path, but it can be accomplished with hard work, discipline, and the American spirit. It is also incredibly rewarding and a great source of pride for those who legally establish themselves as an American citizen.

This country was created by immigrants. Settlers moved to this land and spread all across it in an effort to create a country that allows any freedom that does not trample on the next person's freedom. They were fleeing from countries that controlled their religion, leadership, and business. Many were fleeing persecution, excessive taxation, or a simple lack of opportunity. It is important to acknowledge the creation of our country when we tackle the immigration issue.

Is it fair to enjoy the opportunity that the U.S. has to offer me, a first-generation American, even as I decry those who cross our borders in pursuit of the same? This is an extremely difficult moral question, but one that can be addressed by a sound economic model. The morality of this situation comes from timing. When our nation was first settled, those who entered this land were offered nothing but opportunity and

freedom. They could do what they wanted and worship freely.
Nothing was built, no government was in place, no military
protection was provided, and there was no safety net. These
were the conditions and the survivors of this harsh
environment framed this nation. They allowed others to join
them and were instrumental in constructing the strongest
economy in the world. Now the citizens of this country are
responsible for maintaining that strength.

This is why immigration laws exist. They are a compromise
between permitting foreigners to relocate here while limiting
the expense to existing Americans. Our strength only grows
by bringing in quality individuals from other countries. There
are a lot of brilliant and hardworking people who can only
reach their full potential by moving to a free nation like the
United States. The reality of the immigration issue is that
many of these talented people are going to be denied access
to our business culture and higher education because of the
expense of our illegal immigrants. For our country to reach its
full potential, we must carefully monitor the illegal
immigration issue and correct it to make room for the
immigrants that want to come to America through the proper
channels.

What are the expenses to our taxpayers caused by illegal
immigration? The first issue is the loss in tax revenue
associated with non-documented workers. Most illegals who
work receive their payments in cash and manage to keep their
earnings off the record. Without paying taxes, an illegal

immigrant can maintain a reasonable quality of life on a smaller paycheck. An employer could pay someone "off of the books" 70% – 80% of what they would have to pay a taxpayer for that worker to see a similar net wage. This is also a great argument for lower taxation. Hiring an illegal worker not only eliminates the tax revenue generated by their job, but could also drive up the unemployment payments for the legal citizens as they are being replaced.

The other costs are more direct to the taxpayer. Public education is a large expense. Classrooms have more students, free lunches increase, more text books are required (along with other resources) and bilingual services continue to grow. Healthcare is impacted through the American mandate that anyone entering an emergency room must be treated. Illegal immigrants are not turned away, and their bill still must be paid, in one form or another, for by the taxpayers of the state. Prisons are crowded and there are expenses that span the entire legal process. This includes detention, legal proceedings, interpreters, public defenders, and imprisonment. There is also large scale gang involvement that creates added work for police departments. Through incarceration, education, and healthcare, illegal immigrants create a huge expense our country.

So, how do we handle it? Arizona is making strides toward immigration reform with some unique legislation. They are requiring immigrants to keep papers on them that prove their citizenship. Reasonable searches such as traffic stops and other routine legal questioning are the key means to identify illegal immigrants. If the person in question cannot prove that he or she is a legal citizen, then that person will be deported. It is a way to enforce current immigration laws. No law has any merit if it cannot be properly enforced.

Of course, this has caused huge controversy throughout the nation and the opposition must be addressed. Is this racial profiling? Probably. Most proper police work involves some form of profiling. If a policeman is outrun by a suspect, then it may make sense to start looking for people that fit a more athletic profile. It is also reasonable to take a close look at people with a Middle Eastern descent when there is a terrorist threat. When we speak of illegal immigration, it makes sense to examine the Hispanic community—especially the individuals that are unable to speak English. Society invests a high degree of trust in our police officers. They are able to make decisions about when it is appropriate to use a gun and they should be given the same latitude when it comes to questioning someone about their status as a U.S. citizen. Just like anyone given any responsibility, those who abuse that power need to be disciplined and possibly fired.

Another argument against the immigration reform legislation involves increases in racism and harassing legal citizens of Hispanic ancestry. However, the examination of someone's immigration status should be routine. If someone cannot speak English, then it would be prudent to check his or her immigration status. If someone is breaking the law, then it would also make sense to run a background check for other legal run-ins as well as to verify that person's citizenship. An officer should be able to show probable cause in his or her conduct and also prove that it is a part of normal police procedure. Just addressing the portion of the population that do not speak English or are breaking the law would be a worthwhile and substantial start toward immigration reform in this country. If an illegal worker comes into the United States, works, pays taxes, and speaks English, I doubt that their immigration status will ever be questioned.

The law in Arizona is also interesting from the standpoint of a state taking a stance in properly enforcing a federal law. It is clear that there is a major problem with illegal aliens coming through the Mexican-American border. It floods our country with undocumented workers and it allows international crime rings and easy escapes. This issue needs to be addressed. In addition to properly enforcing our current laws, completing the border fencing may be needed. On the other hand, it is not an easy or inexpensive task for several reasons. The economic costs, environmental concerns, and the relationship with our neighbors to the south must all be examined. Fully understanding the total cost-in both dollars and political capital--of such an endeavor is critical before completing such a task.

I do not believe that relations with Mexico will be hurt by building a wall along the border. If it is necessary for our economy, then that should be reasonably understood by the

Mexican leadership. There is also a good chance that it could help prevent some of the drug traffickers that use Mexico as their passage to the United States. Ending the flow of drugs through the country can only help them to control the criminal element (especially the well-funded, trained, and armed criminal element). Both countries need to work together to keep the border safe for visitors and legal immigration. The gangs and drug cartels that set up shop along the border are detrimental to the economies and safety of both nations and a cooperative approach to protecting the borders would dissolve a lot of that crime ring. I believe that the Mexicans can understand our concern and would even help with the implementation of the safety measures and wall assembly. They could even supply some of the soldiers to assist with border patrol.

Many Hispanic citizens have similar views on immigration because they are in the same boat as 99% of all Americans. They either immigrated to this nation or are descendants of other immigrants. They want to keep their hard-earned wages for their families and not waste it through taxes needed to support border jumpers and drug runners. These groups are the only ones hurt by immigration reform (as well as those paid off by these groups to look the other way).

The key is to address this issue from a couple of angles. The first approach is to deport illegal aliens that are caught through legitimate searches. All workers found to not be paying taxes, as well as those employing them, will be fined or deported. Everyone who is caught committing a crime and found to be in this country illegally should also be sent back to their country of origin. I truly believe that these steps will be enough to substantially decrease the burden placed on this country by illegal immigration. Building a wall should be a last resort. Still, if the first plan of attack does not work, then we may very well need to complete some kind of barrier.

Completing a wall across the Mexican border would be a huge project and one that would require a lot of maintenance and supervision. It would clearly require more troops to post along the way as well as watch for people trying to use ladders to get across the top or welding torches and other devices to simply break through the wall itself. Building the wall would be massively expensive and its supervision and upkeep would be a considerable ongoing cost. The other downside to a wall would be its interference with the environment. There are several reasons that the wall could cripple various environmental aspects of the region. The Rio Grande fuels many of its ecosystems. There are migration patterns that run through the region. Stunting access to the river and limiting these patterns could have a detrimental effect. It will be important to survey the area so that we understand the side effects if a wall needs to be built.

The overwhelming decision that must be made is that we desperately need immigration reform and protection for our citizens. It may take a better enforcement effort of current laws, disallowing offspring of illegals to be given citizenship, and possibly the completion of a wall across the border. The expense of these efforts could be great, but it will be far less than the continued expense of our current course. The drug running, gangs, tax evasion, over-crowding in schools, extensive taxing for healthcare costs, and criminal activity can all be limited by proper governance of our current immigration laws as well as proactive efforts to close the border. Using a tactical approach is appropriate to first stop employment of illegal aliens through deporting them and heavily penalizing their employers. We then need to target the criminal element by checking for immigration status when asking for identification when other laws are broken. Finally, if the problem persists, we may need to complete and protect a wall that completely closes illegal entry into this nation.

I feel that the wall is a last resort, but it is a viable option that may need to be utilized. If you have a neighbor that continues to allow his pets and children run through your yard killing the grass, trampling flowers, and causing other damage to your property, then it would be prudent to install a fence. Is this a blatant display of mistrust to your neighbor? Certainly. Nevertheless, if you have tried to diplomatically reason with your neighbor about what is going on and they repeatedly refuse assistance, then you are well within your rights to build on your land. The saying, "good fences make great neighbors" would apply here. Your fence could be expensive, but in the long run, you now have a protected property and can start to mend relations with your neighbor. Mexico will not hold a grudge forever if we build a wall along the border. They may actually grow to appreciate that wall if it means less drug-running and crime along the Rio Grande.

Still, there is a more economical answer. We could bring home the majority of our troops stationed overseas. Many of them are scattered throughout the world and would gladly accept relocation to Texas, Arizona, New Mexico, or California to work the border. We will talk about the general expense of worldwide imperialism later, but there is a significant savings associated with having the majority of your armed forces at home. There are worthwhile battles to be fought along the Mexican border and winning those battles is important for the safety of both nations. There are also many illegal activities that take place along the Gulf and California coasts. We could aid the Coast Guard's efforts by bringing home the majority of our naval vessels as well. As we discussed earlier, there are issues with building a wall. It is expensive to maintain and it creates several environmental hazards. Assigning troops to this area (that are currently deployed in other parts of the world) makes a lot of sense and prevents us from having to entertain less desirable solutions.

Therefore, if we are a Nation of laws and a Nation of immigrants, immigration should occur within a legal framework, not through the machinations of illegal schemes and scams that threaten our national security.

-J.D. Hayworth

Chapter 8:

Drill Baby, Drill!

Powering our nation has been a concern from the moment we moved away from candlelight into the electric and industrial age. As a developing nation, we started using fossil fuels such as coal and timber to power our progress. It was vital to have an element available to us with a little more kick than what could be provided by an ox or mule. We moved away from physical labor for power and started using natural resources. Today's energy is still dominated by fossil fuels. In addition to coal and wood, we rely predominately on petroleum with heavy usage of natural gas.

Our current energy system is fragile and needs more attention and focus from our leadership. The first problem is that using fossil fuels is incredibly dirty and bad for the environment. We rely on it so much that we actually do not produce our nation's required energy and are dependent on foreign assistance. Also, we are depleting resources that replenish themselves at a much slower rate than what we require to keep the supply constant. In fact, many of them are non-renewable and will be completely drained at some point.

Oil dominates the world's energy requirement and it is in high demand everywhere, but especially here in the United States. We use it for many different industrial processes and require it to move our automobiles. With that said, our usage of oil is not out of preference, but necessity. Petroleum is a highly undesirable fossil fuel because it is filthy and expensive. We have witnessed firsthand the hazards of oil within our own bodies of water. There is still evidence of the 1989 Exxon Valdez spill, and more recently, the BP spill in the Gulf of Mexico will take decades to clean and repair. There have also been colossal spills all over the world. Kuwait and Saudi Arabia, Mexico, and Uzbekistan have all have much larger spills than the Exxon Valdez. The Persian Gulf and the Gulf of Oman are horribly polluted and are probably beyond repair.

The environmental results of off-shore drilling and transportation are evident, but the expense of oil dependence may be more damaging. We conduct business with a part of the world holding a virtual monopoly over an item that we use in record setting quantities every year. If this situation does not give you a mild feeling of discomfort, then factor in the general attitude in the Middle East of pure hatred for the United States and you have a recipe for disaster. We are literally fueling nations that are developing the means to destroy us. The day that we can leave the Middle East with no further use for anything this region has to offer will be a day that strengthens this nation for generations. We will no longer contribute to their military advancement or petroleum collusion. The only hope is that this day comes sooner rather than later.

Anyone can identify a problem, but the real key to advancement is finding the solution. Are there cleaner energy solutions that can provide equivalent levels of power without breaking the bank? This is a tough question. Oil is available and is used in every possible part of our everyday lives. It is somewhat affordable and provides jobs for many Americans. Its use requires no change and that is really where oil gets its strength. It is simply easier for everyone to not change.

For the United States, the first step to solving our energy crisis is to mine our reserves that are on dry land. These are fairly plentiful and much easier to contain in the event of some kind of leak. This is not a permanent solution, but it is a start. We have reserves in Alaska, throughout the Dakotas and eastern Montana, as well as in the Rockies. It is projected that some of these spots carry more oil than several Middle Eastern nations. With our new fracking methods, this is a very exciting time in the exploration for energy. We need to carefully drill these regions to lessen and eliminate our dependence on foreign oil. Once we prove that we can provide our own oil, we will undoubtedly see the foreign sales price for petroleum drop. The drawback of a policy like this is that it brings more of the extraction effort to our home soil and presents the risk of more pollution. Drilling and transportation over land is a much better option than over water, but the environmental concern still needs to be addressed. Nevertheless, this is only a short-term solution.

With this being a bridge between our current situation and a permanent solution, we need to state an actual goal for our country. We have the resources to move to 25% renewable resources in 25 years, 50% in 50 years, 75% in 75 years, and being completely powered by energy sources that no longer deplete our natural resources in 100 years. The goal should be to have a clean energy source that is affordable and renewable. Energy is a national concern and a valid use of tax dollars. Rewarding companies and individuals that make strides toward eliminating our use for oil should be provided through tax breaks. America must make energy efficiency and independence a national priority. The government needs to be in charge of the allowed oil usage limitations, but the private sector must drive the technology advancement. Oil companies will have to shift their focus toward our new goal to survive or risk continued losses and becoming completely obsolete in the next century. My feeling is that the first 25 years will be incredibly tough, but our total transition to renewable resources would be complete in far less than 100 years. The key is to simply get the ball rolling. There would then be an exponential growth in our technology as we continued to move toward our goal.

With oil reserves in this country remaining a bit of a mystery at this point, we may need to supplement them with other energy sources. We must also be careful in examining the alternatives that are available. Our next most commonly used resource is natural gas. We are fairly self-sufficient when it comes to the usage of natural gas, but do import a consistently increasing amount each year. Natural gas seems to be a good alternative right now because it burns much more cleanly than oil or coal. Both of these elements are more complex and tend to release more polluting elements into the air when burned. Natural gas mostly releases water vapor and carbon dioxide. However, it does carry other risks. Natural gas is very flammable with its high concentration of methane. It does require drilling and this process can damage the environment and requires vast amounts of water. Natural gas must also be transported through pipes and this can be a logistical issue. Trying to constantly maintain the lines and monitoring ruptures is another problem.

Another energy resource that we have is coal. Coal is generally frowned upon because of its environmental pollutants and rightfully so. Coal releases huge amounts of sulfur dioxide and nitrogen oxide as well as mercury and carbon dioxide. Breathing the waste product of coal can lead to serious respiratory problems. Power plants also require vast amounts of water to run. The reason to consider coal is that it is incredibly cheap. It is the most plentiful fossil fuel and the United States actually exports more of it than we use. There has been some advancement in filtering burns as well as progress in trying to liquefy it in an effort to use coal more cleanly. Still, coal is a tough alternative and can only be used in moderation.

One of the more recent steps we have taken toward clean, renewable energy is looking at nuclear power. We have men and women splitting the atom to create energy. It is continuously renewable and emits very low gas contaminants that could potentially contribute to the Greenhouse Effect. The major concern about nuclear power is a disaster similar to what happened at Three Mile Island or at Chernobyl. The radiation affects can last for 100 million years or longer. There are also waste concerns under normal circumstances and generally these byproducts are buried underground as there is really no approved method for their disposal. We also have fairly open borders right now and there is always a security issue when nuclear reactors become more and more common.

Nuclear power is far from perfect right now, but it is still in its infancy. We successfully use it in some places around the country and have adapted it for submarines. There is potential for nuclear power and we need to invest into finding whether or not it is a viable source for our future energy supply.

There are some contenders when it comes to renewable energy. We have used water power for centuries and most recently through the construction of dams. This method accounts for almost half the renewable energy that is created in the United States. Solar, geothermal, and wind power all have potential, but they are not heavily used in our society. They require more attention going forward because they are all very clean and come from endless resources. The problem is that most renewable resources currently lack the kick required to really compete with fossil fuels. Hydroelectric power is really the only clean renewable resource that has been integrated into our society. It is clear that further development is needed in these areas because they are the future power sources for our country. Fossil fuels will not be around forever and the sooner we start concentrating on planning for their departure, the better we will be prepared for it.

As an economist, I have the luxury of advising that scientists find a clean, renewable form of energy without any real regard to figuring out how to do it. The government will have to direct this effort by setting goals and limiting the depletion of our natural resources. Our major energy and oil companies will need to start moving their focus to more of a long-term solution. Depending on the Middle East is a huge mistake and grows more costly each year. We have made some initial efforts to harness alternative fuels with nuclear, hydroelectric, solar, wind, and geothermal power. These sources must continue to be cultivated until we come up with a permanent mix of energy producers. Furthermore, while working on this process, I have no doubt that the brilliant minds of this country will come up with something incredible.

The release of atomic energy has not created a new problem. It has merely made more urgent the necessity of solving an existing one.

-Albert Einstein

Chapter 9:

Let It Ride

The gaming and gambling industry has had a profound effect on the economy for a very long time. The United States has typically been tolerant of gambling, but with close regulation. This mix of emotions about the industry started with our early settlers. Puritans came to the New World to get away from the moral corruption of their own countries. They outlawed dice and cards right along with dancing and singing. Still, gambling is not so different from taking the risk of crossing the Atlantic Ocean to explore a foreign land. It became a common practice for many settlers and was a means to socialize with your friends and family after the long work of the day had been completed.

The colonies received a great deal of their initial funding from lotteries. This practice was not unlike the twentieth century practice of selling war bonds. It was your patriotic duty to contribute to your country's exploration efforts. The lotteries were successful in sending funds to the New World and constructed many houses, churches, schools and other structures. In fact, William and Mary, Harvard, Yale, and Princeton were started from lottery funding. Still, as time went on and America gained her independence, the lottery system began to take a different shape. They became extremely corrupt and eventually all states banned lotteries completely. Louisiana was able to restart a lottery within the state, but it, too, was eventually disbanded because of rampant corruption.

In the 1960s, attitudes about running a state lottery started to take a completely different form. Rising taxes lessened the opposition that many states had toward restarting a lottery system. All kinds of public projects from renovations to hospitals and roads could now be funded by the lottery and were not completely dependent on tax revenue. Today, the various lotteries across the nation have an enormous impact on the economy of each state. Most use a part of the funds toward schools. Typical costs associated with schools come in the form of teacher salaries, equipment, building and repair costs, and other day-to-day expenses. With the lottery in place, other programs have become affordable and gained in popularity across the nation. It is now much easier to pay for special education classes, gifted classes, Advanced Placement examinations, child day care services, and many other academic programs. Of course, the most noticeable influence by the lottery on education comes in the form of scholarships for community colleges and state universities.

In addition to school funding, lottery money is used for many other programs throughout each state. Pennsylvania is a unique case in that it uses the majority of its proceeds on care for the elderly. Assistance is provided for transportation, pharmaceuticals, senior centers, meals, and rebates on taxes and rent. Iowa uses funds to assist with tourism costs and veterans. New York has used lottery money to repair and build canals, streets, churches, ferries, and bridges. With the vast amount of money that comes through a state lottery system, there are just as many ways to spend it.

There are still several states that choose to not conduct a lottery. They may take moral exception to gambling and they may also look into the past corruption of the practice. In general, religions are intolerant of most forms of gambling and you can find a consistency with this belief through your more religious states in the southern Bible Belt and Utah. Many also believe that gambling can be addictive and that a lottery preys on the poor and uneducated. It is a regressive tax that only targets the people looking to escape an impossible financial situation, but who are incapable of understand the odds. Of course, this is an opinion and I cannot imagine that there are too many people who truly believe that they will actually win the lottery. Maybe, I am wrong.

I like the lottery format of this nation. It is a great example of how many of our laws and programs should be run. It does not face the burden of trying to protect people from themselves. It is simply a decision that is made at the state level. If your state would rather pay a little extra in taxes or not spend as much on social programs, then that is your choice. You still have to balance the budget and should not be forced to install a lottery. Nonetheless, if it makes economic sense for your state and you have no moral hang-ups with this form of gambling, then you will certainly see an influx of funds to the state's treasury.

Even though lotteries were the first format that put gambling on a scale that had an effect on the economy, the more traditional casinos were not far behind it. The adventurous spirit of the early settlers had many of them moving west to explore new lands. They had money and were greeted by a series of riverboats up and down the Mississippi River that were willing to test their gaming skills. These floating casinos would match them with other wealthy travelers and, of course, professional gamblers. These skilled players would prey on novice gamblers and made a living from playing cards. This group of people was not thought of very highly as many of them were involved in different schemes, cheats, and other crimes.

The lack of regulations in the new frontier of the West allowed gambling to become extremely aggressive. There were also more people heading that direction because of the Gold Rush. These migrations lead to a criminal element that grew with the population. In the early 1900s, most gambling was outlawed in California and this led to its establishment in Nevada. Horse racing also grew in popularity during this time and it had its own share of manipulation.

As corruption grew in the gaming industry, many states completely prohibited gambling of any kind. Still, new laws did not stop it completely as it started to move underground. States found that they had made a mistake and that it was better to have regulated gambling rather than gaming run by mobsters. Still, once the underground element began to work, it was impossible to stop. A combination of legalized gambling with organized crime gave birth to Las Vegas. Interestingly enough, prostitution and gambling have both become legalized business in the state of Nevada. It seems that laws put into place to protect people from themselves rarely stand the test of time.

Even though Las Vegas is the most recognized spot to gamble in this country, it is certainly not the only one. Native American casinos can be found all over the nation and have an interesting history and economic impact in their own regard. They are taxed a little differently than other casinos and do not quite leave the same mark on our national treasury as the Las Vegas casinos. Las Vegas pulls in $10-$20 billion annually and this means a nice tax bill for Uncle Sam. Not only are the profits taxed, but employees pay income taxes, and winners at the casinos also pay on their earnings. Indian casinos are not able to completely avoid taxes, but the burden is much more affordable. Casinos built on reservation land pay the least amount in taxes.

In 1976, Justice William Brennan determined that the United States had no authority to tax Indians on Indian reservations. Furthermore, the country had no authority to regulate activity on the lands. This was an invitation for Native Americans to run with gambling operations. The first developments were high-stakes bingo and lotteries. The appeal to the public came from games running constantly and offering higher rewards. In the 1980's, poker was added to many bingo halls and became wildly popular in casinos. Soon to follow were racing, sports betting, and the more traditional casino games that you see today. These different ventures bring in huge cash revenues ($10-$15 billion annually) and they avoid a large portion of the taxation that other casinos and businesses pay each year.

Casinos on reservation lands do not completely avoid all taxation. Some casinos grow and make deals and compromises with the states in which they conduct business. This is more of an informal agreement to pay so much on earnings rather than strict taxing. Also, employees of these casinos must pay income taxes. However, tribes are able to avoid many taxes on the actual profits of the casino and that is a practice that should be changed. Anyone operating within the borders of the United States should be subject to the same laws and rules. They are able to freely use public assistance, roads, parks, protection by the military and law enforcement, and any other service provided by the taxpayer. It is reasonable that they would pay the appropriate taxes on revenues earned within the borders of such a wealthy nation.

The key issue with Indian gaming comes from the concept of tribal sovereignty. Should Native Americans have the right to freely maintain their parcels of land with the borders of the United States? Some argue that they should. They were the original settlers of this land and Europeans gradually took the more fertile areas of the country from them as they settled the western hemisphere. The laws, taxes, and other regulations of the U.S. do not apply as long as they stay on their lands and stick to the reservations. This compromise was a poor idea from its inception. A nation must be governed in a uniform manner. Even if states are allowed to make some decisions about their laws and taxes, they are still trumped by anything mandated by the federal government. Allowing sections within a nation to have a separate set of rules from the states is irresponsible and dangerous.

So, what do we do? Native Americans were given lands from the government and it really does not seem fair to take them away because we have a change in heart. I agree. Tribes should maintain ownership of their lands with the rights offered to any owner. They should have the right to transfer the deed to the property and to conduct any business on that land that is allowable by law. Nevertheless, every law and tax regulation must be followed. This nation made a mistake when allowing a separate set of rules for the Native Americans. It was done out of empathy and a simple understanding of what it must be like to be displaced from the homes occupied by your people for thousands of years. Still, as areas were settled, the stronger militaries and the more advanced civilizations prevailed and pulled those that they conquered up with them. Our leaders during this period should have forced Indian assimilation into the country, even if they wanted to grant the deeds to certain lands to them.

Today, Native Americans are the most impoverished of any ethnic group in this country. They suffer from high unemployment, teen pregnancy, teen suicide, and dropping out of school. Putting them on an island that secluded them from the rest of the country may have seemed like an act of generosity at the time, but has evolved into a far worse fate than any hostile take-over would have. Some of the casinos are quite profitable. Yet, most tribes do not participate in the gaming industry. This is a sad state of affairs for this community because we will not disband the reservations and tribal tradition disallows branching out into the surrounding communities.

Indian casinos and traditional casinos appear to be doing very well. They are generally full of people placing bets day and night. They are also continually building new additions.

Nevertheless, one dark cloud that looms on the horizon is Internet gambling. The Internet can be used to do almost anything and offers a wide variety of gambling options. The most popular are online poker, fantasy sports, and sports betting. Of course, any casino game can be duplicated by an online equivalent. This opens an interesting can of worms. Will online gaming put traditional casinos out of business? Would it be better or worse for collecting taxes on gaming transactions? Would Indians be allowed to circumvent online regulations on their gaming sites? The progression of Internet gaming will be interesting to follow as any form of gambling generally brings addiction and corruption with it.

If history has shown us anything, it is that we cannot stop progress. New trends must be addressed and we have to adapt. Internet gaming is here to stay and we need to answer these questions to make sure that it is properly regulated and taxed. Taxes may be a wash, but only time will really tell. There are certainly many cash transactions that take place as gambling occurs all over the nation. I believe that many (if not most) of these transactions are not reported to the IRS. This practice will prove to be much more difficult over the Internet. Electronic copies of everything produced would be difficult to hide or to plead ignorance of their occurrence. It is possible that some casinos will go out of business, but online exposure could also provide an advertisement for a casino or for gambling in general. I believe that the overall tax revenue will increase when traditional casinos are combined with a more developed online network. The Internet site will probably take some business from the brick and mortar establishments, but together, they will have a synergistic effect. Also, gaming administrators will not have to worry about running their operations illegally or offshore.

Gambling will always be a part of our economy and we need to embrace it as a reality. States can decide if the detrimental aspects of the gaming industry are worth banning it entirely. It is a moral judgment call that they will have to make. Still, gambling does not need to be ignored. It is a massive industry and it must be properly regulated and taxed. We will never be able to properly monitor all gambling as a good portion of it is done underground. However, taxing Indian casinos and paying close attention to the online transactions that take place with gaming should combine with traditional casinos to provide quite a bit of tax revenue. It could be a nice way to assist the nation in paying down its debt—though perhaps I am being idealistic as I am sure extra revenues will be thrown into useless government spending. It also promotes a free-will transfer of funds from the public rather than the taking associated with increased taxes.

If you're playing a poker game and you look around the table and can't tell who the sucker is, it's you.

-Paul Newman

Chapter 10:

Interest Rates and the Fed

Studying the impact of the Federal Reserve is an important component for the economy of the United States. We thrive and prosper because of the competitive spirit of our free market, but resort to having an overriding authority when it comes to interest rates. It is a compelling paradox of clashing philosophical ideals between a free market and a design-driven structure. Certainly some aspects of the Fed are important and provide stability to the financial industry, but is manipulating interest rates necessary? This is an interesting question and something that should be addressed when determining exactly what powers need to be removed from the private sector and placed into the hands of the government.

The Federal Reserve is not an independent agency, but it is close. While still under the umbrella of the U.S. government, the Fed does generally turn a profit and deposits that amount into the national treasury at the end of its fiscal year. It can also act on its own without the prior approval or permission of the President or Congress. The Fed is financially independent and does not depend on tax funding for its day-to-day operations. It is able to provide for itself through its market operations and lending. The 12 reserve banks of the Fed work in a similar manner. Each privately owned member bank is required to buy a certain amount of stock in the Federal Reserve Bank within its region. Member banks get a 6% dividend from this stock. This is a bit of a gift for holding the required reserve amount that is unable to earn any kind of interest.

The Federal Reserve has two basic goals: to sustain a level of full employment--roughly a 5% unemployment rate—and to maintain price stability and inflation. The Fed monitors banks and provides rules that they must follow in order to maintain FDIC insurance. This adds a consistency and foundation for the banking industry and a calming effect upon its clientele. The Fed also sets the discount rate at which banks can borrow from them and directs the Fed Funds rate at which banks can borrow from each other. Interest rates rise in times of inflation to slow the economy and drop during recessions to promote lending, spending, and stock market investing. So, while examining whether or not the Fed is necessary, we must study the pros and cons of the institution.

What does the Fed contribute and can we operate an economy without them? This is a tough question because the Federal Reserve does offer several key services to the financial sector. They regulate banks. Commercial banks are required to keep a reserve requirement in their safes to cover withdrawals. Most banks would lend as much of their funds as possible because cash does not earn interest. This is a major conflict of interest for a bank and the Fed holds them accountable to their banking responsibilities. In return, banks can offer FDIC insurance. Now, any account holder gets $250,000 of coverage per bank in the event of that bank's collapse. This is an important feature for American banks because it prevents runs on cash in times of economic stress. Furthermore, banks have an institution that they can use for their banking needs. If a bank falls close to its reserve requirements, then it can borrow money from the Fed. It can also use this method to replenish cash that has been lent to customers. The interest rate that they pay for money from the Fed is less than the interest rate they charge for commercial and private lending. This creates the bank's spread. The Fed clears checks and monitors the transfer of money from bank to bank. The U.S. treasury uses the checking services of the Fed and holds a virtual checking account for its own securities, including treasury bonds, bills, and notes.

With such important duties on its plate, what would be the benefit of eliminating the Fed? Milton Friedman criticized several aspects of the Fed, but his major issue fell with their manipulation of a potentially free market. He also had his reservations with giving someone as much power over an economy as is held by the Fed Chairman. There is a lot on the line that depends on the decisions of this individual.

Friedman was also concerned with inflation and deflation. He felt that a growing economy should be guided by a consistently growing money supply, and that this process should be left to a mathematical formula rather than a group of appointed watchmen. He wanted to completely abolish fractional reserve banking (banks would now hold 100% of all deposits) and pay off the national debt so that we could discontinue wasting tax dollars on the interest. This would be quite a change for the banking industry and the overall money supply. Perhaps the most interesting change is a severing of lending practices from the bank's normal duties. This would now only be conducted by separate institutions and not by banks.

Friedman's concerns with the Federal Reserve revolve around its power and influence. He obviously trusted the free market to make more consistent decisions. Furthermore, there are few checks and balances for the Fed. It really does not answer to anyone and is not required to be completely transparent with its operations. So maybe the next step is to audit the Federal Reserve. It makes sense to keep an eye on an organization this powerful, especially one that does not have an elected membership. The Fed can currently be investigated, but the movement to actually audit them faces challenges from certain limitations that are in place. The Federal Reserve cannot be questioned about international banking and investing (both private and government). They also have immunity from inquisitions about deliberations and decisions about monetary policy at home. This would include moves in interest rates and changes to the banking reserve requirements. On-site examinations are also prohibited.

Some have argued that the Fed missed the boat regarding Social Security, welfare, healthcare, the housing crisis and every other economic struggle in this country since 1913. The truth is that its very existence creates the illusion that the Federal Reserve will warn our decision makers about economic crises. This does not need to be the case. The Fed is no more of an economic expert than anyone else. Simply having the chairman grant his or her blessing to economic policy is incredibly dangerous. No one person should have the title (or carry the albatross) of being the economic authority of this nation. It is an impossible job and the predictions will be no more accurate than any weatherman trying to predict the beginning and end of a storm. The perception that the Fed and its chairman have total control over the economy and that anyone can guide the market is foolish.

Like the government, the Federal Reserve does have its place. It is a necessary part of our economy (at least for now) and removing it would be like doing a cannonball into an unknown body of water. The more prudent approach would be to wade out gently and take a careful measure of what happens. If we later find that the water will support a cannonball, then let the splashing commence. Any government institution that is found unnecessary should be disbanded immediately. Still, the Fed is so ingrained into our economic system that it will take a while to figure out just how necessary it really is.

The first alteration needs to be in the form of discontinuing interest rate manipulation. The market can handle this without any government involvement. Supply and demand work amazingly well and need no help from the Federal Reserve. The basic open market operations are the part of the Fed that overstep the bounds for government involvement in the market place. Like minimum wage and rent controls, moving interest rates interferes with the free market and has negative long-term consequences. Many argue that the Great Depression was drawn out much longer than it had to be because of poor decisions made by the Fed. Letting the free market work through the recession would have been a much less painful process.

The key to running a stable market is consistency. People need to be comfortable with its concept and its reliability to reflect what the market wants. If rates are low, we now have two possible reasons for that position. We could be in a situation where deposits are high and banks are holding a lot of cash. They need to lend more money and rates are reflecting that need. The Fed confuses the matter because they can set artificially low rates when they feel that the market needs stimulation. They pass money to banks in an effort to create growth in the economy through lending and replenishing those funds.

This causes a number of long-term problems. We now have confusion in the marketplace. People may feel that the economy is in a downturn because adjusting interest rates is a reflection of the Fed's opinion of the market. It could also mean that the Fed feels that our debt is getting expensive and keeping rates low is the only way to combat that problem (assuming that actually paying it off is not on the table). This mechanism also causes inflation and penalizes Americans that have actually saved money. Taking the Fed out of this equation altogether would mean only one thing. People would see low rates as part of the business cycle. They would also deduce that high rates mean only that banks are low on cash and are offering this incentive to raise funds and discourage people from pulling cash from their reserves.

Dr. Ron Paul has been a long-time advocate of auditing the Fed and has had considerable success in gaining support for this notion. Unfortunately, his bills have never quite made it completely through the filter of Congress either through dilution or simply not passing. Regardless of these challenges, it is to be hoped this will merely be a temporary setback for a much-needed change in our nation's financial operation. Many of the lending decisions of this nation are a direct reflection of our leaders having entirely too much power. Pushing banks to lend to people with poor credit, to lend too much to those who do qualify, and to then bail out banks that fail as a result is an incredibly dangerous practice. It makes properly functioning companies slaves to the government. Washington is slowly able to control private enterprise and direct tax dollars to companies that would fail otherwise because of their poor management.

The Fed is simply becoming another conduit for government control over the private sector and it is time to list exactly what is expected of the Fed and what limitations they have to obey. The protective side of the Fed is really the most useful characteristic of this institution. FDIC insurance creates a consistency and level of comfort among bank depositors. Also, regulating banks and ensuring that they are dutifully carrying out their non-money making duties is vital. This generally means making the bank adhere to a 10% or higher reserve requirement. In exchange, the bank gets to list FDIC insurance on CDs, savings/money market accounts, and checking accounts. This insurance is a key to building confidence within the banking system in the United States and allows business to continue to run in the face of a recession that might otherwise cause panic.

The Fed needs to stop at this point. They have no business interfering in the private sector. The government does not need to direct lending in any fashion. Forcing loans and creating artificial interest rates have had large detrimental long-term effects on inflation and they create financial bubbles. Milton Friedman may have been right about taking the lending instrument away from banks, but I believe that our current system can work with a few adjustments. One key argument about the government not being involved in lending is that banks will run out of cash to lend for housing and this will drive up interest rates. This may be true. Housing could be an exception to the rule and it may make sense for the government to buy mortgages. With Fannie Mae and Freddie Mac showing a huge ineptness to handle this kind of arrangement, banks may need to simplify this system and carry all of their own loans. This gives the institution a direct responsibility to manage their own loan portfolio and keeps their interests aligned with their risk. Buying a house is a major decision for the borrower and the lender and the entire process has become entirely too lax in this country.

Furthermore, having an entity that lends to banks that intend to relend that money is a problem. It creates inflation instantly and keeps the money presses rolling at an incredible rate. Lending among financial institutions already exists and is a market that can work on its own. The Fed can oversee all normal lending practices among banks and make sure that the financial institutions that participate are not breaking the law by colluding and forming monopolies. This is the most economically sound role of the Fed. They need to be an insurer and a regulator. Once an entity is given these powers with the freedom to operate in the business world, they create a problem for the American people by creating a huge conflict of interest. Certain powers need to be stripped from the Fed, but following through with Dr. Paul's audit is the first step.

A great industrial nation is controlled by its system of credit. Our system of credit is concentrated in the hands of a few men. We have come to be one of the worst ruled, one of the most completely controlled and dominated governments in the world--no longer a government of free opinion, no longer a government by conviction and vote of the majority, but a government by the opinion and duress of small groups of dominant men.

     -Woodrow Wilson

Chapter 11:

Race Relations and Political Correctness

The first step toward actually developing a society of equals is to simply treat everyone equally. Resentment builds when different people are given a different set of rules. That contributes to prejudice just as much as ignorance. The key to uniting people is to give them the same opportunity without providing assistance. Affirmative action, equal housing lending, differing admission standards, hiring quotas and other means of manipulating free enterprise may be more detrimental than they appear at the surface. It is important to take a true look at their impact and figure out if our efforts in the advancement of disadvantaged people are really working.

Affirmative Action, like most social policies, comes from a sound and caring ideal. It is a means of advancing people that have had to deal with a history of discrimination. This movement would include the promotion of women and minorities in the areas of business and education. The main purpose is to proactively examine situations where groups and classes of people get into ruts that turn into generational cycles. Affirmative Action is the attempt to move these groups forward and present opportunities that would not normally be available to them, thereby breaking that cycle. Many countries around the world practice some form of this movement and it generally applies to women, minorities, people with disabilities, and aboriginal or native people. They receive preferential treatment when it comes to entrance exams and requirements as well as quotas that are set for hiring. Malaysia and South Africa actually have policies like this in place for the majority in their respective countries due to past discrimination.

In most polls, minorities are for Affirmative Action while the majority is not and that correlation should probably be assumed. Still, there are several arguments against this practice that should be examined. Does someone deserve the same praise for an accomplishment if they have an easier hurdle? The devaluing of the accomplishment is not the only slight. Giving certain groups a lower standard identifies these particular groups as unworthy and incapable of success without a little extra help. This qualification can potentially develop into resentment from those looking to hire, promote, or admit to a school. The simple task of finding the best person for the job mutates into a game of making the percentages add up correctly. Meeting the quota becomes just as important as finding the right personnel.

Thomas Sowell had some interesting results from his study of Affirmative Action. He found that the system has been diluted a bit by anyone that did not fit the white male majority profile. When women and immigrants were included, this practice actually now covered most of all Americans. Immigrants also do not have a direct link to past discrimination, but have made their way onto the approved list.

Sowell feels that the advancement of black people has less to do with Affirmative Action than with their own determination and work ethic. He asserts that people initially developed because of geographical position and through travel. Societies that went to new lands learned the most by taking ideas from other cultures and incorporating advancements that they did not have into their own lands. He further comments that when a government starts to act as the savior of a certain race or gender that they actually have a very opposite effect. He believes that the government creates classes through these rules. For example, by bussing black students across town to a white school, he asserts that the government is basically labeling the school in the black community as substandard.

The private sector being free from the regulations of Affirmative Action may make a little more sense to most businessmen because of the competitive nature of the U.S. market place. They need to hire the best person for the job regardless of race or gender in order to put together the most effective product or service that they can offer. On the other hand, should this competitive nature also appear in the public school system and in the college ranks? Students that come from families that have not previously pursued higher education may not be as supportive of this endeavor or not know the procedure. It can be overwhelming to acquire application documents, pay for achievement tests, have transcripts sent, or even know what classes and extra-curricular activities are attractive to colleges. There are also issues with prep schools having low funding that may not provide the same advantages as other school districts. Furthermore, non-English speaking homes may have a more difficult time cultivating reading and writing skills for their children.

Advocates for Affirmative Action would also advise that colleges accept a wide variety of people. Like Sowell mentioned earlier, cultures with exposure to other cultures prosper the most. Lowering admission standards for certain groups is an attempt to make up for a disadvantaged system. The idea with all of this is that if all races are given the same academic opportunities, then you will see advancement by minorities. Eventually, it will lead to a more competitive race and give everyone a virtually even starting point.

A lot of this approach comes from a reasonable perspective, but there are some issues that arise with a program like this. The first thought that comes to mind is that there will be a general resentment toward a race that has preferential treatment. They will be seen as unable to achieve a goal that is set at everyone else's level. College is competitive and taking the very best applicant, regardless of race, will build the best overall student body. It is also possible to build a diverse student body by factoring extra-curricular activities into the evaluation process. Bringing in students with a background in sports, debate, student government, foreign language, charity, and many other activities can make an incredibly diverse group. You also run the risk of reverse discrimination where a person may have better qualifications, but is not allowed admission because a spot is taken by someone meeting a quota. Lowering standards for minorities also does more for wealthy individuals of that race by creating better opportunities for them. The poorest of each race can still be neglected by Affirmative Action.

So, what actually happens when the free market takes over and applicants are left to their own devices? Well, it would be naïve of me to claim that businesses and schools will be fair and equal in their hiring and admitting of women and minorities. In both of these circumstances, there are only a few people who will be making the decisions and people make mistakes. They may miss the best candidate because they do not evaluate them correctly, are not thorough enough, or even because they are prejudiced against a certain race or gender. Regardless, this does not necessarily mean that the free system has failed. It means that there is a huge opportunity for a competitor to step in and scoop up the best candidate. Competition brings out the best in everyone and it makes each team in the game try to accumulate the best possible players, even if that player is a different sex or race. Discrimination is a flawed practice, but it should not create legal issues for a company or university. If they limit their applicant base for any reason, then they will miss out on a lot of very good people and, over time, will begin to fall behind others that integrate or use fairer methods.

An excellent demonstration of this very idea comes from a gentleman named Sam Cunningham. He was an African American running back for the University of Southern California in the early 70's and was named an All-American during his college career. He took on Southern football god Bear Bryant and the University of Alabama in Birmingham in 1970. Most accounts of this story paint a picture of a Southern football coach who had been challenged by the FBI about integration. However, even the most progressive person could understand the pressures on Bryant to maintain an all-white team in the state of Alabama during this time.

Nevertheless, the performance of Sam "Bam" Cunningham changed some minds that day. USC crushed the Crimson Tide and a lot of their dominance was a product of the performance of Cunningham. Allegedly, Coach Bryant pulled him into the Alabama locker-room after the game and told his team, "This is what a football player looks like." The University of Alabama would soon integrate the football team. This was not a result of a newfound respect for every man regardless of race. They simply wanted to win.

Winning is the only real goal that mandates a level playing field. Teams and businesses that want to be the best have to hire the best. Sometimes the best can be the less accomplished individual. This may sound a bit contradictory to the rest of this chapter, but I will clarify the point. If someone comes from an impoverished background and shows promise through hard work that is well above that of his or her peers, then that person should receive strong consideration. To continue the sports analogy, it is the same as the NBA drafting a player that is big, strong, and incredibly athletic, but who was never really coached properly through their early basketball career. A manager may want to take a flyer because of their huge upside potential. Another example of this would be taking a student with good test scores and grades from a school that averages much lower marks. That person probably has much higher upside potential than the "C" student who is surrounded by college-bound peers because of his or her relative success.

The issue (like most) cannot be addressed by the government. Forcing schools and companies to hire under-qualified people is simply ridiculous. Competition provides plenty of incentive to put together a great team while not discriminating. As I mentioned earlier, the company or school that does not admit or hire based on race or sex is putting themselves at a disadvantage and are setting the stage for a competitor to conquer them. Government interference in the private sector generally causes long-term problems and programs to help the disadvantaged are no different. This not only includes Affirmative Action, but equal housing lending and even rent controls can be added to the list of long-term failures caused by manipulation of the free market.

Both concepts come from well-intentioned beliefs, but suffer in their application. We have talked about the failure of the housing market because of lowered lending standards. However, is *equal lending* the same thing? Discrimination in home lending is strictly prohibited by the Department of Housing and Urban Development. Essentially, for a bank to enjoy the foundation of FDIC insurance, they must adhere to the equal housing rules set forth by the Fair Housing Act of 1968. Lowered lending standards were a simple manipulation of the intent and wording of this act. It was never intended to present opportunities to some that were not enjoyed by others. It was to serve only to eliminate race, gender, religion, etc. from being included among lending requirements. This deviation of the document's intent led to one of the biggest financial crises in American history.

So, is equal housing lending necessary? As a former bank lender, I can honestly say that is completely superfluous. The days of going into a cigar-smoke filled office to beg and plead your case for a loan are finished. Still, like most laws, the government has not adapted to the system as quickly as the free market. Most banks have a virtually automated system. A customer comes in for a loan, the loan officer assists them with the application and it is sent to the actual decision maker who processes the credit score, payment history, income statements, etc. to make an approval call. This person rarely meets the client and has no way of know the applicant's race, heritage, sexual orientation, etc.

Most banks require that loan officers take applications if a customer wants to provide one. I had an experience where a customer came into the bank every week to apply for a loan. It did not matter that the bank had turned him down 100 times before his current visit. He knew that if he was turned away before submitting an application that he might have grounds to sue the bank. So we kept taking the application and following up to let him know that it had been denied-- *again*. This was a hassle and there was no way around that, but it was a requirement by my employer. I also did not get paid per application, but rather, by the number of loans approved and so it was not financially beneficial either. This was a situation where I valued my job and just hoped that the man would hit the lottery and all of my hard work would pay off one day.

That scenario was fairly uncommon. Many different types of people came into the bank to apply for a loan and there was no way for me to guess at a glance whether or not they would be approved. Most lenders were trying to make the most money that they could and that meant sending up applications for anyone that could "fog a mirror." I did not care what your background was, if you wanted a loan, I was going to try and make it happen because it would positively affect my paycheck. As the only person that met the client face-to-face, I had no authority to screen anyone. The person with this responsibility simply got an application number with all of the pertinent information to take out a loan. He or she would then evaluate this information against the bank's lending criteria to see if the customer would be approved. It is a simple process and a great way to let only the facts determine the outcome without bringing into question the issue of discrimination.

Race relations and the issue of political correctness come down to a simple issue of respect and individual responsibility. If everyone is on the same playing field, and one person is beaten out by another, then healthy competition is present and working. If a person gets a position because of race or background then that situation will naturally breed resentment. If you take that agenda further and start taxing one group to pay for the advancement of another, then you are really going to start stirring a race relations problem. The government is actually driving racism and inequality by setting very distinct limitations and goals for different segments of the population. Men and women of different backgrounds, races, and nationalities are never going to start comingling if they are seen and treated differently by their shared government. It is difficult to consider someone a valuable equal if they have a different set of standards than yourself. The time has come to put everyone on the same playing field so that the slow process of civil equality can start forming.

Excellence is the best deterrent to racism or sexism.

-Oprah Winfrey

Chapter 12:

Live and Let Live

Because I am a Christian, this is a difficult chapter to write and I know it will generally cause disagreement with most of my more conservative contemporaries. Still, I do believe that this nation needs a bit of a make-over when it comes to enforcing values. We were formed as a union that was very much intent upon leaving men to their own devices. The original settlers of this country had many different ideals and purposes for coming to the new land. They may have wanted freedom from oppressive taxation, freedom to worship, or simply the unlimited potential for growth and success. The draw of America was the fundamental understanding that one could enjoy the freedom of this country with the only boundary being the point at which your freedoms interfered with someone else's. It embodied the adage of "as long as I'm not hurting anybody," then you were free to do what you wanted.

It is not the government's place to enforce values. There are a great number of issues that come up for debate each year that are judgment calls that must be based on the values and background of the person trying to make a decision. Gay rights, racial and religious profiling, welfare and social security, foreign aid, the death penalty, prayer in schools, drug use, and progressive taxation are all decisions that are made with some kind of moral directive. Government decisions need to be carefully examined, but rarely considered if they infringe on someone else's rights. The first area that is typically taken for granted is the government's taxing. Taxing is an infringement and should only be used when absolutely necessary. Protecting the nation with a military is a necessity and unavoidable expense. Making sure that everyone has their personal needs met is a judgment call and not a legitimate reason to tax the people.

The first point to analyze is the difference between charity and taxing for charitable purposes. I hear the question, "how can you deny someone healthcare, housing, and education and still call yourself a Christian?" quite frequently. Contributing to charitable causes is something that should be done on an individual basis. It is not up to the government to fund charities. Charities are well run and pinch every penny. They need to be run privately to maximize efficiency. The government is wasteful and takes advantage of charities by using them to pay for voters. A candidate will offer legal bribes to people in hope of securing their vote, and that has created a significant conflict of interest. Forcing increases in taxes to fund charitable organizations is a hefty assumption when the entire populace does not share the same set of fundamental ideals. There are also many people who resent the taxes they pay in this category because they want the freedom to choose where their charitable donations go. I am one of those people. My participation in my charity of choice (Big Brothers Big Sisters of Middle Tennessee) would increase in frequency and in depth if some of my tax burden were lifted. I now do what I can, but my budget does dictate the level of my participation.

So how would we determine what is a reasonable expense and what is an unnecessary use of tax dollars? To some extent, you will have to make a judgment call based on alternatives. Using this method should lead to better decisions than trying to assert your personal values. For instance, should we tax the American people to support the military and pay for the care of the disabled? You can find people on either side of the fence for both issues. If you examine what the country would be like if we had a privately run military or one that was not funded through tax dollars, then it is easy to see how weak the alternative would leave us. Paying for the care of the disabled is a value-based choice as well. The alternative would be to revoke funding and let private charities pick up the programs.

If this did not work, then it is hard to expect the truly disabled to take care of themselves. Careful funding in these areas is more reasonable because the alternatives are limited and unattractive.

So, what is the difference between the unattractive alternatives for discontinuing funding for the disabled and discontinuing funding for unemployment or welfare? The one glaring difference is that the truly disabled do not have the ability to make a living and provide for themselves adequately. Unemployment benefits are not an evil and can really save individuals who lose their job through no fault of their own. Nonetheless, two years of unemployment benefits is a waste of tax dollars. People still need to take personal responsibility for their actions and play the hand that they are dealt. It may not be easy or as advantageous as someone else's situation, but it is still their life to live. Welfare is similar. People who are physically able to work have the alternative of getting a job. Many of them choose to stay home and have children that they cannot afford. Paying for this lifestyle is the worst alternative because it removes incentives and taxes the working people in this country. It also encourages behaviors that are disadvantageous to the United States.

Gay rights are an interesting case as well and are probably the easiest example of legislation being put into place to implement a moral agenda. There is no real reason to prevent homosexuals from marrying or from adopting outside of religious doctrine. A married couple has several advantages legally and when filing taxes, and it is against the spirit of this country to disallow the union of gays. It is not the federal government's place to make a decision on this issue. This is situation that it easily settled by a live and let live mentality. We are currently violating the rights of homosexuals in this country to please the morals of others. This combination creates a federal issue instead of a judgment call that should be left in the hands of individual states.

Now, if letting gays marry is not enough to completely destroy the moral fabric of our country (just kidding), then letting them adopt should also be reasonable. It seems odd that we, as a society, are more comfortable with an institution that has constant turnover and inconsistent funding taking care of unwanted children than we are of handing them over to a well-screened, gay couple. If sexual orientation were taken out of the equation, most conservatives would probably agree that a child would have a better future if raised in a loving home rather than some kind of orphanage. It is more reasonable to put children in a private home rather than a public institution (at least I am consistent when it comes to public and private). We need to realize that religion should have no bearing on legislation in this country. It is a slippery slope. More social conservatives would probably agree with this sentiment if they took a look at demographic changes and the direction in which this country is moving. In the not-too-distant future, we will be predominately Catholic and in the long run, there is a strong possibility that we will be mostly

Muslim. For this reason, it is going to be important (especially for Christians) to be consistent with our laws and to form precedents that do not have religious bearing. This should also apply to adoption. By that logic, the current screening system should remain in place and set the same standards that a straight couple would have to maintain in their home.

Gun owners should be afforded the same rights and privileges as well. We are lucky that our forefathers were forward thinking enough to see that owning firearms would come under fire at some point in the future. This is where the Second Amendment has become extremely valuable. It is the right of responsible adults to own a gun. It can give the person a feeling of security, a means to hunt, and a method of defending themselves against attackers (including their own government or if there is a call for conscription). These people are not the general concern for gun control. Of course, having the ability to own a gun does give an attacker or criminal a better means to get what they want.

The first step to fighting this problem was to create laws. We have laws against sawed-off shotguns, against felons owning guns, mandating waiting periods, as well as registration and transportation mandates. Many of these laws are the result of the gangster era. There is an interesting law in Kennesaw, Georgia that requires the head of each household to own a gun and ammunition. This unique law is credited with an immediate drop in crime of 89% in the city, and for the maintenance of the lowest crime level (for a city its size) in the whole country. In 2007, Kennesaw enjoyed its 25th straight year of being a murder free city. You simply cannot argue with the results.

I am not an advocate of forcing people to do anything. I would prefer people to have the right to choose. Everyone should be considered a responsible adult until they prove otherwise. The saying, "once you outlaw guns, only outlaws will have guns" carries a lot of truth. It is important for the good guys to have the right to own a gun because it is most certain that those breaking the law will have them. Protection from invasion is another intent of the Second Amendment. The Japanese were reluctant to attack the continental United States during World War II because two-thirds of Americans owned a gun.

In almost every situation examined, gun ownership lowers crime. States that are more gun friendly and that allow the concealed carrying of guns have significantly lower crime rates than states with more strenuous laws. Switzerland is an interesting study because they require conscription from all able-bodied young men. They are required to serve in the military, where they are taught to shoot. They are then required to keep a firearm and ammunition in their houses in case they are called upon later to serve. Once again, you have situation where having firearms in the home has produced a low-crime environment. Just for the record, I do not own a gun and do not have one in my home. Nevertheless, I do appreciate my right to have one and respect the rights of gun owners. I am sure that most gun owners are ok with my decision to not own one--even the people of Kennesaw and Switzerland.

The theme of this chapter is personal choice and the protection of our individual liberties. Honestly, I should have no moral say over your actions, just as you should have no say over mine. The United States was created with this idea at its very foundation. The Democrats in leadership positions need to learn to live within their own means when it comes to the national budget. It is unreasonable and irresponsible to expect taxation to alleviate your concerns regarding work, children, food, shelter, and retirement. Taxes devoted to these areas are violating the rights of the working class.

The Republicans in leadership positions needs to get away from pushing moral and religious doctrine. There is no place for morality in government. We will be more efficient with quantitative laws, not qualitative. It is not the government's place to comment on homosexuality, abortions, drug use, or anything else that does not directly affect you—and hurting your sense of morality does not count. If morality is going to be imposed by law, then it is only appropriate it be done at the state level; even then, it needs to be in moderation. It is a bit odd that Republicans do not see a correlation between big government and pushing a moral agenda because they are one and the same. It is time to stay out of people's lives and let them be. Freedom only works if you get out of the way, and that goes for both parties.

Democrats can never get any sleep because they are afraid somebody somewhere is making too much money.
Republicans can never get any sleep because they are afraid somebody somewhere is having too much fun.

-Anonymous

Chapter 13:

The Tax Man

It is a shame that the only universal truths are death and taxes. Taxes, by their very nature, are an assault on the working class. They have practical uses for goods and services that can be tough to maintain privately, like roads and defense. Still, taxes are a burden not only to those who pay them, but to an economy that grows through the efforts and funding of its best entrepreneurs. Taxation is a violation of rights that has become so commonplace that we throw them around without much consideration for the people that are forced to pay them. They are easily corruptible and a manipulative way to get elected. Most people overlook taxation and the government revenue system because it has become so colossally huge. That is an unfortunate comment on our society and an issue that needs to be corrected.

Throughout history, the most common style of taxation was regressive. It existed in the feudal system and was also commonplace in many other societies. The people at the very bottom worked the land and *may* have been able to take enough food from their efforts to provide for their families. They then passed the rest of their earnings to the person who owned the land. That person would pass along a piece to the next person and this would continue up to the king.

We now commonly feel that this was an unjust practice. Still, we do have some programs in place that resemble regressive taxing. A sales tax has been called regressive. If you are strictly looking at basic needs, then buying these items will be less of a percentage burden on a person with a higher income (of course, you do not want to take into account that wealthier people generally buy more expensive necessities). The lottery is relatively regressive because poorer people typically spend a greater portion of their income on tickets. This money is then typically used by the state for education funding (once again, it is virtually impossible to protect someone from themselves).

By its very nature, taxing is going to be unfair. Someone is going to pay more than someone else; either by percentage or actual dollars. A flat tax seems to be a good compromise because everyone pays the same percentage. If a high-income earner pays 15%, then they will be paying more in actual dollars than someone that has a lower income paying the same percentage. During his presidential bid, Steve Forbes was a proponent of a flat tax program and it is really not a bad idea. It makes paying taxes fairer and is a good compromise between liberals and conservatives. Everyone is doing their part and paying something into the system.

So, where did we go wrong? The answer lies in the size of our government. It got too big. Now, the government is expected to police the world, provide housing, provide food, provide for children, protect the moral fabric of our various religions, provide unemployment insurance, and provide for your retirement. This may sound like an expensive grocery list because it is. The reason that we moved into a progressive system is that the so-called conservatives needed money just as the liberals did. It was important to spread our ideals throughout the world as well as to make sure that everyone at home was following them. The very people who were supposed to protect the citizens from over-taxation had converted to the dark side. It is not really shocking to see our level of debt passing $18 trillion in 2014 and still rocketing skyward. The Democrats and Republicans have been working together for years to raise taxes! They may have different agendas and complain about the spending of the other party, but they are both guilty.

The good news is that we are not without the means to recover--*yet*. However, the situation demands attention and it requires a fundamental change in our taxing and spending policies. This means an adjustment to fiscal policy as well as a correction in the way that we pay taxes. The first item to be addressed has to be spending. I do not believe that our economy can entertain higher taxes at this point without squeezing industry and potentially decreasing government revenue. If we stick with the analogy of diet and exercise to lose weight, then I believe that we are working out every day, but eating everything in sight. We have got to cut back on our spending (eating) and it will take a great deal of compromise from both parties to make it happen. Republicans need to agree to bring the troops home (where possible) and quit battling gay marriage. The latter is not necessarily going to help us save money, but it is a reasonable concession that could potentially bring some cooperation from the Democrats.

The Democrats need to understand that the government does not exist to take care of them. Social security, welfare, Medicare, Medicaid, food stamps, and unemployment are all unconstitutional and are morality programs that should be run at the state level. They create an unconstitutional conflict of interest with voters because they promote poverty and encourage support for the candidate that will provide the biggest handout. The states already have responsibility for some of these items, but they need to assume responsibility for all of them (or eliminate the program altogether). Social Security will take some time to wean from the public, but initially, it would be a good idea to move the benefit age back to 80. We cannot afford the current system. It would also be prudent to look at the overall budget and pick through every item of expenditure. We need to evaluate the private alternative and apply the filter of morality. If it pegs on the morality meter, then it is a state issue. I do not even want to think about the nonsense that is tucked away in the federal budget. Without unloading our financial burden, we will never truly be a free country.

Addressing taxes will have to come later when we get spending under control. Unfortunately our bad diet has caused an unhealthy country and the non-stop working out must continue. Getting the annual deficit back into the black would be an amazing first step, but we cannot stop there. We have to be diligent with the cuts and try to maintain our tax revenue. I feel that this is a gross violation of taxpayer rights, but our poor voting has created a mess that we have to clean up before we move forward with tax reform. It would be irresponsible to address the tax issue first. That would be the equivalent of someone making a risky career change while they have a mountain of debt with family obligations. Just as a responsible adult would handle the situation, a responsible country must continue working at an unpleasant job until the debt and budget are under control.

If, by some miracle, we do figure out a way to actually get our political parties to cut spending, we can move on to the tax code. As I have mentioned before, I find taxation to be an abuse of power and an infringement on our rights. It needs to be used in moderation and only when completely necessary. The ideal system would have been to carefully calculate what we were spending and then determine if each expenditure was a vital necessity to the safety of our people and the economy. This seems to be the sticking point where some say that it is vital to make sure that people can retire and vital to make sure that parents have provisions for their children. This is an exaggeration of the letter of the Constitution and never the intent of our nation. The proof is in the personal statements of all of our founding fathers. They all believed in freedom and independence from an oversized government. This was the very reason that states were formed! They were assembled to collect like-minded individuals that could govern themselves and run their own budgets.

I mention this to only make a point about how far we have strayed from our original design. It does not change the predicament that we are currently facing. Yet, it is nice to dream about what our country could be. Let us pretend for a moment that we are now debt free and running a huge surplus because we are still overtaxing our citizens. We now have the ability to change the tax code. I feel a bit like a person that talks about how they are going to spend their lottery winnings right after they buy a fistful of tickets. We are probably talking about a fantasy. Oh well. Taxpayers can be dreamers too, right?

I believe that we have two options and I am happy with either of them. A flat tax is my first thought. The idea has been around for a long time and is a simple method of setting a tax rate and everyone pays the same percentage based on their income. The wealthy pay a bit more from a pure dollar perspective, but everyone pays the same percentage. It is important to have everyone pay into the system. You have to take ownership of something to show it the respect and care it deserves. Our nation is no different. This is why I believe that you should only have representation through taxation. If you are a net loss to the United States government (excluding military personnel of course) then you should forfeit your right to vote. You can have it back as soon as you begin to participate in the system. When everyone pays, they have some skin in the game and you now have a series of owners that are making very careful decisions about what is best for this nation.

Our second option is the fair tax. This is a taxation system that applies a sales tax that is used to run the government. Your income is no longer taxed. You take home everything that you earn (speaking to those who are not self-employed) and simply pay taxes when you buy something. This would be my choice for a couple of reasons. Firstly, it gives the taxpayer some prerogative as to when they would like to pay their taxes. If things are tight, then you can cut back on your spending and also keep more of what you earn to pay your debts. On the other hand, if the economy is booming and people are spending money, then the IRS can take advantage of that situation to fill the coffers for a rainy day (or to use on science, education, medical research, etc.).

The fair tax also gives us the ability to tax the wealthy. There is a huge segment of the population that pays very little in taxes, but has an enormous amount of wealth. These are people that acquired their wealth early and live off of the income that it provides. This success could be through early business profits or even an inheritance. Warren Buffet often talks about paying a lower tax rate than his secretary. Of course, it is important to understand that he has already paid taxes on the money that he uses for income. He is simply paying the lower capital gains rate on his investment income while his well-paid secretary is paying the higher income tax rate.

If we were to move to the fair tax system, Buffet and his secretary would probably pay a similar rate because his spending would now be taxed. If conservatives were to pitch a tax change to liberals, this would be the way to do it. Demonstrating that you have found a method to tax the wealthy, non-working populace would probably be appealing to them. You need to think like a politician sometimes! Please note that my goal is not to attack the wealthy with taxes. Still, I do believe that the working class is the most critical piece of any economy and needs to be protected. A correctly run government at the proper size would lower everyone's tax rate. In that case, a fair or flat tax would work equally well.

I give another edge to the fair tax because it also taxes income earners that do not pay what they should. There are people engaging in illegal activity who naturally do not pay taxes. Regardless, drug dealers do spend money, and the fair tax would take advantage of that. You also have people that fudge the numbers from a corporate level and business owners that take allowances that are improper. This taxing program is the best idea that I have studied to get everyone involved and make sure that we are all paying into the system.

My common theme of simplicity really sticks its head out when discussing taxation. We waste a ton of time and resources preparing, paying, and auditing taxes. We complicate an unpleasant part of life and it is completely unnecessary. If you are charging an affordable amount of taxes, then you do not need to provide tax breaks. If you buy a house, have a child, or run your own business, then you need plan it around the tax structure. Adding deductions and exceptions drives up costs and that in turn drives up the amount that must be paid in taxes. Pick a rate, and then tax spending or consumption at that rate. Make it easy and understandable. This idea keeps waste to a minimum and allows everyone to have a better understanding of their financial situation.

Our financial lives can be better. Taxes were not written into any document by our founding fathers. There is no reason to have a law or any other requirement that your life should be a total wreck throughout the spring. If we simplify our government and our tax code, then the lives of the working class will improve. They will be able to plan for the future more accurately and follow their own personal budgets with more diligence. This overhaul is long overdue and it is time to start protecting the working class against a government drag. Of course, we could always start assessing taxes based on your voting record. I would be held responsible for my fair share of the military, education, and science. Conversely, a liberal voter and taxpayer would be held responsible for Social Security, Medicaid, Medicare, food stamps, unemployment, welfare.... Seems fair, right?

Every diminution of the public burdens arising from taxation gives to individual enterprise increased power and furnishes to all the members of our happy confederacy new motives for patriotic affection and support.

-Andrew Jackson

Chapter 14:

Climate Change

Global warming and climate change are a combined issue that has evolved over the years to encompass several different environmental concerns. The assumption and hypothesis is that the earth is warming because of volcanic eruptions, plate tectonics, and several other occurrences. However, the focus of this movement is to study mankind and the effect that we are having on the earth. It is clear that we do pollute our surroundings in different ways. The debate is over the severity of damage we are causing to the planet. Conservatives generally feel that the impact is minimal and liberals estimate that we are causing our own destruction.

The cause for alarm (as I understand it) is the warming of the earth due to the absorption of too much heat from the sun. Essentially, we are eroding our own atmosphere because of pollution and this is weakening the walls designed by nature to protect us from the harmful direct rays of the sun. This is reflected in several different aspects of our life. For humans, it can cause an increased frequency of skin cancer because of the higher concentration and impact from exposure. It also would cause warming of the oceans and land. This could lead to icecaps melting and waters rising as they expand. There are many other side effects, but I believe these to be the most immediate and direct concerns.

So, is this happening? Are we causing so much pollution that we are going to cause our own deaths and the destruction of our planet? It is estimated that over the last 100 years, the earth's average temperature has increased by about 1.5 degrees. That does not sound like much, but you can see that, over time, we could have a problem from a trend like that. The heat could eventually cause part of, or the entire world to become uninhabitable through the gradual increase of water levels, deserts, and temperatures conducive to the human condition. The key is going to be to evaluate earthly conditions over a long time frame to see if recent patterns are significantly different from normal fluctuations in temperatures throughout history.

The first determination needs to be a focus on what is a long-term and permanent change versus a short-term anomaly.

The Medieval Warming Period is one such anomaly that took place from approximately 950-1250 AD. It is basically impossible to know what the specifics were during this period because of limited record keeping and communication, but there were several odd occurrences that took place during this time. The Vikings took advantage of the warmer climate to navigate seas that had formerly been blocked by ice. They were able to travel and colonize Greenland and Newfoundland. North America has some historical findings that correlate to the warmth of Alaska and Canada and how it related to the migration of Native Americans. Many developed nations do have some indication that there was a spike in the overall temperature that they experienced during this timeframe.

Consequently, from the 16th to 19th century, the earth entertained a cooling period called the Little Ice Age. Being later in time, this period has a bit more documentation to confirm its existence. The Viking settlement in Greenland was wiped out by the cold. Iceland's population took a sharp decrease. Many waterways were also frozen over for extended periods. London's frozen Thames hosted a festival in 1607 and the Swedish army attacked Denmark by marching across the frozen Great Belt. New Yorkers could walk from Staten Island to Manhattan across a frozen New York Harbor in 1780. There are explanations for this cooling cycle as well. Some suggest that the Black Death and its direct impact from decreasing the world's population could have caused a reduction in heat.

I have always had this idea that fluctuations in earthly temperatures were caused by inconsistent or progressing orbits taken by the earth. I thought that I had a brilliant idea (or at least an admirable one for an economist). My assumption was that the giant blue ball was and is flying through space and would not hit the exact spot in the galaxy on November 1st this year as it would November 1st of next year. There had to be some difference in the location (just going with the odds on this one) of the earth in comparison to its distance from the sun. The earth is Icarus and if it ever took a path that got a little closer to the sun than usual (much like someone running the 400 meters out of lane 5 and creeping into lane 2 in the curve) its wings would melt. The overall temperature of the earth would increase. This scenario would also hold true in an opposite fashion if the orbit were to swing wide.

This is a sensible argument; however, I was beaten to it by about 90 years by a Serbian geophysicist named Milutin Milankovitch. He, of course, not only had the idea, but investigated it and comprised several very detailed explanations for how global temperatures work in relation to the earth's orbit. His first idea is that the earth oscillates in a range. They typical shape of a globe (like one that you might have in an office) is close to the angle that the earth uses to rotate as it moves around the sun. The angle (or tilt) changes within a range and that causes a different severity caused by the seasons—warm or hot summer and cold or cool winters. The earth also takes different orbits each year and this theory has been expanded upon by Kepler. The earth has basic reactions to its orientation to the sun and gravitational pulls by Saturn and Jupiter as well as momentum based changes in movement. A child's top, when not perfectly spun or slowing, is a good example of how this works.

I like this study and I think it is equally as convincing as any idea presented about global warming and the pollution caused by humans. Conservatives are often described as anti-science because of their religious beliefs, but there is a segment of that group that does attribute every occurrence as God's will. I am more of a Christian who believes that God gives us free will and a lot of slack. I see science as a way of trying to understand how the world that He created works. Religion and science are not mutually exclusive, but quite the opposite. They are a way to heighten understanding about the world around us.

Why the science lesson in a book trying to correct the economy of our republic? Well, we need to decide if the Greenhouse Effect and global warming are a dire situation that requires immediate attention and funding. My answer would be--*maybe*. There does appear to be potential with this idea. I do not think that anyone believes that the smoke and different chemicals that we pump into our environment are improving our situation. Those practices do present the risk of a negative impact on our surroundings and potential side effects down the road. You can still accept that notion and feel that global warming is a myth. I gave a perfectly reasonable account of what the situation might be and that it is cyclical to some degree.

There are a couple of issues that arise when talking about climate change. First of all, changing the way that people conduct their lives and businesses to lessen the likelihood of global meltdown is expensive. Our national debt presents a problem in this issue as well. We simply cannot afford to do anything about it. The first environmentalist response to me would probably be something along the lines of "How can you not afford to address this?" I would answer that it is not an immediate concern. The trend is moving slowly right now and even if we are doing damage to the planet, it is still taking a long time to impact our lives. I believe that getting our financial house in order is a more pressing concern with real implications in our near future. It would be amazing to move to a place (financially) where we are taxing at a moderate level, but are still diligent enough with our money that we start to build the treasury. Much like a family on a proper budget, our nation would build an emergency fund. This account would allow us to address issues like this, or help out areas of the country that suffer a natural disaster, or help other countries around the world if we wish. We could cut a check to these areas because we are financially stable and do not need to raise debt or taxes.

The second issue that needs to be addressed is just how much damage global warming causes. Generally, warmer temperatures promote life. You have longer growing seasons and more activity in areas that have warmer climates. Of course, it would be reasonable to assume that deserts would expand, but you would have that area replaced by some of the northern regions that have a hard time sustaining much life. This trend certainly could not continue forever, but it is hard to panic about something that may become life threatening in 20,000 years. In the shorter term, you would have people migrating away from some of the warmer areas because they are no longer able to farm and skin cancer would increase in frequency.

What do we do now about global warming and climate change? Democrats want us to address it immediately because we are all going to die. Yet, it is not an immediate concern and we are broke. That will not work. Republicans believe that it does not exist and that we should ignore it. There is evidence that the climate is changing and if we are wrong with this assumption, we will all suffer in the future. That approach also does not work. We have to keep an eye on it. Continue to monitor temperatures, sea levels, and all of the other criteria to determine how things are trending. To ignore the situation would be foolish and to throw a bunch of money at a problem with no real immediate concerns is equally foolish. Let us first get our finances in order and then we can start to invest more heavily in science and education. We have some time.

The danger is that global warming may become self-sustaining, if it has not done so already. The melting of the Arctic and Antarctic ice caps reduces the fraction of solar energy reflected back into space, and so increases the temperature further. Climate change may kill off the Amazon and other rain forests, and so eliminate once one of the main ways in which carbon dioxide is removed from the atmosphere. The rise in sea temperature may trigger the release of large quantities of carbon dioxide, trapped as hydrides on the ocean floor. Both these phenomena would increase the greenhouse effect, and so global warming further. We have to reverse global warming urgently, if we still can.

-Stephen Hawking

Chapter 15:

The Empire Strikes Back

If forced to choose between Republicans and Democrats, I generally side with Republicans because of my affinity for fiscal freedom. Still, I get annoyed with them regularly. It is just not quite as frequent as my disapproval of what the Democrats are doing. Still, one major concern that I have with the GOP comes with military spending. As we spread our military across the globe, it becomes more and more costly to keep each unit properly led and equipped. Armies work best in smaller, efficient groups or squadrons (much like state governments work more efficiently than the federal government). When focusing on fewer units, they get a more appropriate amount of attention as to what they should be doing and how productive and needed their presence actually is. When they are spread thin and divided into many, many groups, we open ourselves up for waste and unnecessary deployment.

The global idea of imperialism flourished when France, Portugal, Spain, and Britain began to colonize the more *savage* parts of the world. They used the new lands that they colonized to bring back valuable goods to their own countries. The powers of the world (basically the countries with the strongest navies) were literally mining their colonies of their valuable resources. When the colonists of Britain figured out that they were meant to provide this same luxury in addition to taxes to the motherland, they lashed out and formed our nation. Our very birth was the result of an aversion to imperialism.

So, am I anti-military? No. I have numerous family members and friends who have served and I am proud and thankful for all of them. The military is a wonderful way to learn a trade and is basically open to any individual that would like to learn something new and improve his or her life. In that regard, the military is a great form of welfare. If you were born into a poor situation, you can offer your services to your country and have several doors opened immediately to you. I have always preferred the idea of giving assistance to those who give something in return and you certainly have to earn your pay when you join the military. It also exposes a person to real leadership, which may be something that he or she did not get in the home.

Regardless, I would far prefer to keep the vast majority of our military at home because I want them to be safe and because I believe in a more traditional application of foreign policy. Right before the Revolutionary War, Thomas Paine wrote *Common Sense*, a 50-page pamphlet that set forth the merits of declaring independence from Great Britain. Paine presented the idea that all men are created equal. This was a shot over the bow of the monarchy. He would not support leadership that was given power without the elected support of the people. Many of the themes of Paine's writing set the standard for our new nation and his revolutionary ideals remained firm for a long time following the War for Independence.

Paine's first idea is that a small area should never rule a larger one, both in land mass and population size. Also, distance is a meaningful division between areas when determining their alliance with one another. The new country, he believed, would be better served to govern itself independently and avoid the alliance politics that were so influential in Europe.

George Washington furthered this policy of isolationism when he became our first president (we honor Washington's military prowess, but his knowledge of government and organization were also impressive). The idea of being a friend to all and an enemy to none without engaging in alliances held fast and had unwavering support from Thomas Jefferson, John Adams, James Madison, and James Monroe. The Monroe Doctrine reinforced this idea and the policy continued with many future presidents. In 1863, the United States declined an invitation to join Napoleon III in his battle with Alexander II of Russia. Our resolve, on the other hand, would not last forever.

In the late 1800s, the US citizens were becoming increasingly aggravated by the treatment of Cuba by the Spanish. It is possible that they saw a similarity to their own plight previously suffered under British rule. The final straw came when an American ship, The Maine, was sunk in Havana Harbor. President William McKinley sent an ultimatum to the Spanish to relinquish control of Cuba and they refused. The might of the US Navy eventually proved to be too much and this lead to the Treaty of Paris in 1898. The US gained temporary controlled of Cuba, and permanent control of Guam and Puerto Rico. We also got involved in the Spanish occupation of the Philippines and (after fighting there as well) were offered a deal to purchase the islands for $20 million.

The global issues of a growing nation started to pull America into different conflicts. The Panama Canal would be an avenue for trade that was in the best interests of our economy. Even as we hit the turn of the century and approached World War I, our economy was threatened by the German submarines that blocked our trade with Europe. We are a country of mostly immigrants and as nationalism grew and atrocities continued in the native lands of many of our citizens, we started to change our focus. We were no longer a country with a priority of peace. The new slogan was "Peace with Honor." Our emergence into global affairs was now underway and it has been an expense that the taxpayer has dragged around for over a century.

Defense spending is now our third biggest expense and it typically keeps up with our largest two annual expenditures, welfare (food stamps, Medicaid, Medicare, etc.) and Social Security. There is only a few billion dollars in difference between the three items and they are all approaching a trillion dollars in annual cost. We currently spend seven times more on our military than the second most costly military, China. Furthermore, US military spending is more than the next 20 highest spending countries combined. It is a massive expense and I believe that it is an easy way for Republicans to show that they are serious about debt reduction. Demanding that social programs be cut without making sacrifices in terms of defense is a poor plan and will only be met with resistance.

We currently have forces deployed in over 150 countries. In general, about 30% of our military is overseas. If maintaining a presence in other countries were not such a high priority, we could bring most of these troops home. This is important for a couple of reasons. It would keep them out of harm's way and closer to their own families, as well as help us save on the various expenses that are associated with having troops away from home. There is high cost associated with having a standing army, but we would save some money because of this withdrawal. Also, we would lay the ground-work for discontinuing foreign aid. It has become far too frequent of an occurrence that the United States is counted upon to police the world and provide humanitarian aid anytime there is a disaster or problem. With our current debt issues, we are in no position to take on such a role.

As mentioned earlier, the US had a basic policy for its first 100 years or so that taxpayer money was not to be used for foreign aid. There were some private organizations and church groups that would send money to various global causes, but we did not proactively have our government tax for that purpose. We got the ball rolling by responding to regions that were ravaged by World War I. The US loaned money to several areas in Europe, but later, most of those loans were forgiven. We also sent aid to Russia as they were struggling with typhus, but of course a lot of that (as is much foreign aid) was politically driven. We targeted areas that were vulnerable to communist ideals.

This theme of financial assistance continued before and throughout World War II. We sent money and military aid to countries that we considered to be vital to the defense of the United States as well as areas that were against the spread of communism. The Lend-Lease program intended to let select countries borrow some of our machinery, ships, etc. with the understanding that we would get them back after the war. We later settled for a repayment on these items rather than their return. However, only about 10% of their value was repaid. The United States spent roughly $50 billion on this program in the early 1940s. The US has a long history of injecting money and munitions into countries that are threatened by communism.

Still, foreign aid can be a worthwhile endeavor. From a historical context, we have helped country after country throughout the world to recover from war, famine, natural and economic disasters. We have provided funding for AIDS research in Africa, money to protect against terrorism throughout the Middle East, and assistance to Israel, one of our biggest allies. For a country that has its financial house in order, foreign aid is a wonderful use of excess resources and a great way to alleviate tensions in volatile parts of the world. With the earning power in the United States, we have the ability to do a lot of good and to help a massive amount of people.

However, we are not currently in a position to exhibit this kind of behavior. We are broken financially and need to focus on fixing our internal problems first. Discontinue foreign aid and bring as many troops home as possible--these two items need to be a proactive goal. Our troops could do a lot of good within our own borders. As previously mentioned, it would benefit us to station troops along the Mexican border to help with the illegal immigration and drug running issues. This is a domestic need and we need to reallocate our resources to address it. We also need to make foreign aid more of a one-time gift. It does not need to be an annual promise for income that goes on forever. We contribute to a need and then that country is expected to pick up the pieces and provide for itself.

It is more affordable for us and it is better for them in the long-run.

The biggest concerns that arise from this sort of move seem to be in the name of national security. There are a lot of people who feel that the humanitarian aid is the primary concern, but that is only seldom the case. We are bribing some countries and occupying others in an effort to limit terrorism and spread democracy. The goal needs to be a strategic withdrawal of all funds and personnel in such a way that it does not cause a military problem for us down the road. This is something that cannot be put into immediate numbers, but must be orchestrated by our leadership who have the military intelligence to know exactly what moves will put us in harm's way.

Other than simply adding troops to combat the crimes that take place on the Mexican border, there are other benefits and points to consider. We have a top-notch missile defense system. We spend anywhere from $2 billion to $4 billion annually to maintain it and that defense mechanism can take down any projectile that originates from North Korea or Iran (or anywhere else) before it crosses our borders. Our missile defense is not intended to stop an all-out assault from an advanced nation, but it is sufficient in protecting us from a terrorist cell that gets its hands on a nuclear weapon and figures out a way to launch it. Making sure that we have a presence in every communist or Islamic country is a bit of an overkill and a misappropriation of funds. This system is adequate and would allow us to withdraw from some of the more violent areas that we currently occupy.

Running a standing army is expensive even if most of the troops are in your home country. Still, we would trim a little off of the national budget by making this move. Like many obsolete laws, we have troops stationed in areas with outdated missions. Some countries view us as the world's police and we would do ourselves a lot of good to exit several points of occupation to attempt to remove that title. It would display a trust in their own leadership and people as well as letting them know that we do not intend to meddle in their political affairs forever. The goodwill attained from our humanitarian efforts is minimal and generally short-lived. Military and financial deployments need to have a specific objective and when that objective is completed; both forms of assistance should be withdrawn.

The age of imperialism needs to end. Many great civilizations have fallen throughout history because they spread themselves thin by trying to police the entire known world. We are really no different. The United States has resources strewn all over the world and it is an expense that we could drastically reduce. The importance of meddling for the purpose of self-preservation is a bit overstated. We should keep all of our embassies and continue to work and communicate with all foreign countries and trading partners. The key is to let them be and allow them to rise and fall on their own accord. Providing humanitarian aid and manipulating governments is a costly affair and the financial and military benefits from that practice are minimal.

Foreign aid might be defined as a transfer from poor people in rich countries to rich people in poor countries.

-Douglas Casey

Chapter 16:

Government Created Wealth

As much as we demonize many wealthy components of our society, the government has an instrumental position in creating that very wealth. When moving away from a free-market system, it becomes easier to work behind the scenes to create faux value. In the laissez-faire approach, value and utility are rewarded through profits. When a need is met, a winner is made. Conversely, as the government grows and offers various programs, the value is clouded and winners are created artificially. It is important to point out some of the winners that are propped through legislation rather than their own merit.

As mentioned before, casinos are big business. They are beautiful buildings and seem to be growing bigger and more immaculate every year. I do not doubt that they would be incredible enterprises on their own. Nonetheless, they do have government system that gives an almost exponential boost to this industry. I will explain.

The elderly segment of the population is predisposed to gambling addiction. According to the AARP, older citizens can be drawn toward casinos because it provides excitement to a person that may be lonely (because of alienation by their children or after losing their spouse). As any good business would do, casinos know their clientele and will cater their methods to attract more of that demographic. They have senior benefits like reduced meals or free bussing that is used to get them in the door. Once there, they gamble all day and then take their complimentary ride home. It becomes an escape for many older folks.

This section is not about the dangers of gambling or the need to protect certain people from them. It is, though, an examination into an industry and why it is becoming more focused on that segment of the population. There are a couple of reasons—time and money. Seniors generally have both. In this country, we have made the choice to take care of our seniors through Social Security. It enables them to stop working and take government assistance to finish out their twilight years. This combination has created the perfect gambler. Free time and free money provide the motivation to head to the casino. The growth of the elderly population into the target consumer market of the gambling community is increasing rapidly. Retirees currently constitute between 25% and 33% of all visitors. This is really amazing when you take into account the difficulties the elderly may have with transportation and the fact that many of them are no longer working and probably live on some kind of fixed budget. The gambling establishments have taken care of the first problem while the taxpayers assist with the second one.

Looking at the numbers and demographics makes this a more intriguing topic. Social Security will easily exceed $1 trillion annually in its expense over the next decade. We are already in the $800 billion range annually, but as Baby Boomers retire and our life expectancy increases, Social Security costs will skyrocket. This system was originally designed to force us to save for our own retirement, but we have basically killed the original program and now pay for it out of the general tax fund. This is certainly a concern, but also a huge opportunity and growing market for the gaming industry. There are going to be loads of senior citizens with a great deal of free time and tax dollars on hand. For many, gambling will be a normal allotment of this stream of revenue and a budgeted part of their everyday lives. It is safe to assume that casinos will continue to grow and build newer and even more amazing facilities. The elderly lady with the oxygen tank is a staple customer and she is going to be a major focus for future marketing. With this, you can expect a considerable amount of Social Security tax to eventually make its way to Las Vegas, Tunica, and Atlantic City.

The gaming industry is not the only business that can attribute its success indirectly to government action. Oil lobbying has revolved around $50 to $175 million annually in spending. The industry is feeling constant pressure to evolve, but has found a way to remain, for the most part, intact. It has been successful in exerting political pressure in several different areas to keep profits flowing. Lobbying, by its very nature, is a way of influencing an overbearing government. After all, what good would a lobbyist be if there were no higher power to give him what he wanted? Oil companies (and many other industries) take advantage of the size of our government to prop up an industry that should probably be dead by now. Oil production is a filthy process that pollutes everything it touches. It is also an unsustainable resource. We should have moved forward long ago with a real effort to address our energy needs, but that has not been the case.

The push to find an energy technology that can power a home or a car outside of using oil is not new. It is, nonetheless, fighting a major battle against our government to gain traction. There have been some successes where public sentiment and the private sector pushed through the red tape. Electric cars are slowly becoming a real alternative. There have been many ideas through the years that have been purchased and squashed by the oil companies. Still, my major concern is with the efforts of the government to slow progress

162

and allow energy to proceed as it always has and without evolution. This is another situation where proponents of big government dislike *Big Oil*. Ironically, the size of their government has made it possible for *Big Oil* to not only remain intact, but also continue to grow. This is where voting is vitally important to the future of our country. If you notice that a Republican and Democrat are both receiving funding from the same source, a red flag should immediately be raised.

This sort of operation spans many types of businesses. It is not difficult to look at the biggest companies in the country and examine the stress that they put on the taxpayer. Wal-Mart is an easy target for this type of misuse, but it is hard to criticize them as they are certainly a taxpayer themselves. Regardless, they do take advantage of many government programs. That practice creates an inefficient circulation of money and a considerable amount of deadweight loss. Wal-Mart is able to generate wealth by subsidizing their operations through tax dollars.

It is a cycle where taxpayers get *lower prices* on goods because America's largest retailer underpays its employees (according to normal supply and demand) and puts stress on their suppliers because they are basically a monopoly. When they flex their muscles and force suppliers to cut them a deal (because you do have to sell through Wal-Mart) the suppliers underpay their employees. This causes the people that work for these various businesses to make less money than they ordinarily would.

How does Wal-Mart (and many other companies) make this possible? They simply make it a regular practice to work at this company and still use food stamps and Medicaid. Wal-Mart will even help you learn the system and apply for the program! Please know that I am not bashing any company that runs this type of scheme. It makes sound business sense and it enables you to take advantage of some of the tax money that you spend. The problem comes from the big government program. Offering so many people food stamps and Medicaid makes this practice possible. If these folks were not eligible for government assistance, Wal-Mart would pay their employees more and take the burden off of the taxpayer. We create the low prices because we are subsidizing them and alleviating some of their overhead cost.

This is not a new process. As long as there has been government, there has been government abuse. Many of our programs are run with good intentions, but they lead to misallocations and economic inefficiencies. The idealistic approach to government is not the problem, but rather the assured corruption that occurs as a government grows. As the state grows, so grows waste and the opportunity to skim tax dollars here and there without anyone noticing.

There are legendary stories about $100,000 toilets and $800 hammers. Private citizens are the best stewards of their own money. Government officials are far less concerned about stretching the dollar when they are receiving funding from someone else. The key to run idealistic programs is oversight.

They must be run at the state level (as opposed to federally) because they can be monitored, applied and altered as needed. Propping major business with tax dollars is just another unnecessary expense of the hard working citizens of this country.

Every year the Federal Government wastes billions of dollars as a result of overpayments of government agencies, misuse of government credit cards, abuse of the Federal entitlement programs, and the mismanagement of the Federal bureaucracy.

-Chris Chocola

Chapter 17:

The Do Over

When I was younger, if something happened to interrupt a baseball or football game, we would call a *do over*. This might occur if someone caught a pass right by the sideline or if we had a ball bounce too close to the foul line to make a correct call. We would just act like the previous play did not happen and would replay it. Of course, taking this kind of approach with the economy is completely inappropriate and unreasonable. Nevertheless, I am just writing a book. This is not policy and I am not bound by the constraints of pleasing everyone or always making a reasonable argument (even though I do try my best most of the time). So, let us pretend for a moment that we can just wipe out our debt and existing laws. We want to create an economic platform that would be fundamentally sound and conducive to growing business as well as attracting the very best people the world has to offer.

We now have an economically clean country and the ability to do anything we want with the budget and taxes. How exciting! This is a similar situation to what our founding fathers had in 1776. I think they did an amazing job of laying the groundwork for how our country should work. I am in no way criticizing their accomplishments or ideas. Since the day the Constitution was written, we have looked for loopholes in their documentation and used these ambiguous areas to stretch their ideas to mean something different as well as to push various agendas. We need to find a more concrete way to get back to what these great men had in mind for this country. Combing through our laws to make them more concrete and less open to interpretation would be incredible.

So, let us deviate a bit from the theme of this book. Previously, we have discussed ways to make adjustments to struggling economic systems. Instead of making small corrections here and there utilizing compromise, let us just rule with an iron fist and make wholesale changes. I think you will find that most economists like to talk in extremes because it helps them to drive home their points. I am not different. If you want to see the possibilities that could result from a trend, then extrapolate what is happening to the biggest degree. That will give you your answer and provide the concerns that need to be addressed. So, even if many of the items we discuss are impossible to implement, let us take a look at them anyway because it can be a useful exercise.

First of all, we need to put together a tax plan that is lasting and economically sound. It needs to be able to drive the very necessities of this country as well as promote business growth. My concerns about taxation have been covered, but it basically comes down to a fear of driving away wealthy citizens and discouraging businesses from growing. Both are in jeopardy when taxes are raised. The progressive tax is difficult to maintain because it is a tax on income. The more appropriate way to tax would be to focus on spending and using more of a fair taxation style. This would make sure that everyone contributes to the system. This rate needs to be low, in the 5% range. Remember that the federal government will only be in charge of a few things here and there and it should not take an overwhelming amount of revenue to keep it running.

Life would be a little different from the normal disappearing direct deposit that we have all become accustomed to throughout our working lives. We now keep all of it. Every dollar we earn gets deposited into our bank account. (You no longer write off 401(k) contributions, but we will talk about that later). Awesome, huh? This is a huge advantage for every citizen. You have a distinctly new element of control over your life and budget because you can have some say in how much you will pay in taxes. If you are pinching pennies and saving, you will be rewarded because you will compound that effort through your tax savings. If you are doing very well or have enormous wealth, you will pay taxes on your purchases and a growing economy will fill the coffers of the treasury. We are now moving the burden of paying for this country from the workers to the spenders. The key difference in these two groups is that there are some major spenders in this country that do not earn an income. We no longer have to worry about the tax evasion from offshore accounts, money acquired through illegal activity, or any other loophole.

Many politicians would cringe when reading everything above this sentence. They want to have a set (or growing) amount of money to spend each year. We currently use a system where there is a predetermined amount of tax revenue allocated to different projects and necessities. If that money is not used in its entirety that year, then they will receive less the following year. This encourages anyone receiving public funding to burn through every bit of money they receive, even when it is unnecessary.

Shrinking the government and moving to a fixed budget with a fair tax will remedy most of that issue. Firstly, we will be able to audit our government programs better because there will not be so many of them. We can analyze what was spent and what was accomplished to determine if future spending is necessary. Waste will also be reduced further because there is only so much money available through taxation. If we find that something needs additional funding, then we will either have to pull from a surplus or from another program that is not as important. It should go without saying that our new country will require the federal government to run a balanced budget.

Taxation should be simplistic and unburdening to the point that accountants are no longer needed. You pay a simple tax when you make purchases and do not write off anything. If you want to buy a house, run a business, or have a child, then plan accordingly. Taxation should not be used to push agenda or reward behavior. It should be just a small issue that funds the small needs of a properly run government.

With that said, I do admire people in the accounting profession. They are tedious, detailed, and put in more time and pay more attention to their clients' specific situations than most other occupations. They are usually highly skilled and intelligent, and we are wasting these talented individuals. I do not believe that it would be difficult for them to find other jobs and they would certainly be instrumental in moving this country forward through their work. The same cannot be said about preparing taxes and I would love to see a reallocation of this portion of the workforce.

The fair tax would have some amazing long-term benefits. Companies and individuals from all over the world would be interested in setting up shop in the United States if they intended to drive a business. They would be able to hire locally because taxation would not be added to their bottom line. That would make the productive workers here that much more attractive. The great minds that are oppressed all over the world would flock to this country to have the freedom to learn and explore without a meddlesome government. The sky would be the limit and it would be incredible to see how high this country could soar when you remove the lead weight of an income-tax.

Would states counter a small federal government by growing their own? Maybe. That is their option. If they want to provide for the homeless, benefits to the unemployed, retirement, housing, etc., then they have the option to raise taxes and pay for these items. Some states will pick up some of these programs and run them more efficiently because they are lead on a smaller scale. Still, other states will choose not to participate in such programs. Citizens will have the choice to live in their current state or move somewhere that falls in line with their ideals about taxation and social protection. Personally, I would not want to live in a high tax state that offers a safety net for every possible risk in your life, but I do support the option of a state to choose its own path. They have to balance their budget and if they can do that by taxing their citizens, then that is perfectly acceptable.

The theme of this country needs to be liberty and freedom. You should be able to do anything you want until it infringes on the liberty and freedom of someone else. A little competition between the states will not hurt either. We can examine the states that are prosperous and compare them to the states that consistently struggle with their budgets.

This idea is not only reserved for the fiscal laws of this country, but needs to be extended to the social ones as well. In my new republic, no federal laws will exist that make a morality judgment call. States will handle that. Abortion, drinking, gay marriage, gambling, drug use, running a radar detector, and anything else that is simply of no concern to the person next to you would fall into that category. The states will decide what they do and do not find acceptable. You will see many areas adopt certain laws and many of them would fall in line with their moral compass. The South and Midwest would be more likely to ban most (if not all) of the social issues listed above. They would also probably run only a few social programs and have lower taxes. It would be interesting to see how the economies of the different states develop as they choose their separate paths.

The question then becomes what to do with our tax write-offs. We can claim all sorts of different liabilities and expenses against our taxes that will help with the burden that taxation creates. When we tax spending, it becomes much more difficult to do this. Write-offs would effectively end. Decisions would now have to be made based on your own personal life. If you want to have a child, then that is wonderful. You pay for it. If you want to have a house, then you are responsible for its costs. Running a business, donating to charity, investment losses, and the many other ways that you can lessen your tax burden would be eliminated.

From most fiscal conservatives, I don't think I would get much resistance on this idea. It is such a big improvement over our current system that it would be easy to overlook the write-offs. Regardless, I would expect some raised eyebrows about the business expenses. This particular write-off encourages growth and the entrepreneurial spirit. I agree (when working within the constraints of our current tax system). Just keep in mind that taxes are going to be so low that paying them will not be an enormous burden. I feel that our new system will be so business friendly that the economy will flourish and expenditures will be more efficient. They will now only put money into ideas and capital that are felt to advance the mission of the business. Currently, taxation is a major determinate for where a business should invest. That needs to be eliminated. The time and money saved from not preparing tax documents will also go a long way for any busy business owner.

The key for this country is a bit of regression. We need to move back to being one of the more economically free countries in the world. The United States is still in a better situation than most. Yet, there are several contenders now that have lower taxes and more economic freedom. They will close the gap and eventually pass us if we maintain our economic course. We have to realize that we are not better or smarter than anyone else in the world. Our advantage has always been our economic freedom. That has been the straw stirring the drink for this country from inception. It has encouraged growth and has allowed us to pluck great minds from all over the world because so many were attracted to the American Dream and freedom.

Simplicity also needs to be a more common theme. We try to outthink ourselves sometimes. Many ideas look feasible on paper, but they have negative long-term consequences. So, our new republic is going to provide for that potential problem with a couple of alterations. First, all new laws and taxes will expire after two years. If they are working, then we can extend the law. If not, then we just let them expire and move along or make the necessary adjustments where the law is currently lacking. This would put an automated auditing system into effect to make sure that any changes made to the country are positive. Only time can give us a definitive answer on how effective or impactful a change will be. Each law needs to go through this probationary period. It is really not even necessary to make the laws permanent. Many, like Social Security, take decades before they become a national burden.

The second change that we can make is for Congress to have an annual spring-cleaning for our current laws. For one month each year, we comb through all of our existing federal laws (and states should do the same, but that is their choice) to see which ones are obsolete or ineffective. No new laws should be passed during this time. It is strictly reserved for eliminating poor legislation. I equate this to repairing an old home. You can always slap on a new coat of paint or add a new appliance to make it more attractive. Nevertheless, if you want it to be a solid, long-term structure, then the owner needs to explore the crawl space and pull out the rotten boards. He needs to pull out the old heating system and replace it. Wiring, lead-based paint, and duct work all need to be examined. Laws get old and outdated. They need to be changed with the times. Some of them are so entrenched in our current legislation that we need to make the occasional effort to examine them and their long-term viability. Over time, this will create an efficient and effective set of laws that are much simpler to follow.

This will have another positive impact. Many legislators are hired over and over again because of their experience and knowledge of our system. I like the idea that any person can be elected and make a difference without political experience creating a hurdle in a voter's decision. Anyone should be able to come into office as a rookie and make an impact without having to learn the process. So, an older retread Congressman that berates a younger challenger because of their lack of understanding about *how things work* would become a moot point. A voter should only vote for someone that shares their ideals and not worry about how effective that person will be because of their years of connections.

The proper theme for our country is a lot like the proper theme for our economy. It is virtually impossible to legislate morality and proper conduct. You can penalize it and offer disciplinary measures, but taking away guns or redistributing wealth will never cure the normal faults of mankind. The difference with our government is that we can pick and choose among the populace to find quality people to represent us. The root of all good actions is having a good person at the core. That is why voting is critically important and why compromising your vote to the lesser evil is a disservice to your fellow citizens. Our leaders need to be the very best people that we have to offer because a government cannot be great without solid individuals working in it. This is evident throughout history. Countries that were able to string together great leaders had the longest periods of prosperity. This expectation cannot be legislated. It has to be carefully screened and elected.

It is difficult and probably unreasonable to elect quality people consistently. We never really know everything about a candidate. We simply vote on their public image and hope for the best. That is why it is important to leave most decisions to the free market and only involve the government when it is absolutely necessary. A bad apple (or even a whole bunch of them) will undoubtedly make his or her way into Congress. It is important that their powers are limited and that checks and balances, as well as a reasonable level of turnover are in place. The economy can struggle to overcome poor leadership with unlimited power. However, it rarely experiences positive, long-term benefits from excessive regulation and laws. Most government meetings should take the basic approach of discussing how to handle a problem by allowing the free market to manage it. Government involvement should be an absolute last resort. We do not want to be in a situation where our livelihood depends on the people leading the country. If this is the case, then we will undoubtedly fall at some point, just like every other great empire throughout history.

Being a leader is not easy. It means that you have separated yourself from your peers and that difference will automatically make you a target for criticism. You have to be bold with your convictions and continue to act on your beliefs, despite all of the contempt you may receive from others. Free market capitalists hear words like uncaring, hateful, ruthless, and selfish to describe our methods. Still, these are judgments by world leaders that find themselves in a different situation or by pandering politicians that are buying votes.

We should be proud of the fact that an economically free country provides the greatest opportunity for all of our citizens. It does not matter how poor you are at birth. Everyone has the chance to prosper in an economy that lightly taxes and regulates only when absolutely necessary. This opportunity is available to anyone who wants to take advantage of it. An economy littered with social programs is an anchor to drag by the working class and creates a ceiling of limited opportunity to those receiving assistance. There are many, many countries in which to live if you share this philosophy, but we have to realize that being a little different is okay. It has made us the world power that we are today and it has given us the continually attainable American Dream.

I am an outspoken advocate of paying large amounts of income taxes—at low rates.

   -Warren Buffett

Acknowledgments

The completion of this project would not have happened without the assistance of many wonderful people. My amazing wife, Lyrad, supports all of my crazy hobbies and projects. She was even on board when I told her that my first offer to publish this book included a $15,000 fee. I love her very much and am lucky to have her.

I want to thank my incredible editor. Susan Woodhouse walked me through all of my rookie questions, including why spending money to publish this book would be insane. My writing is only legible because of her efforts.

My Aunt Susie Vass Gal assisted with my fact checking, especially in regard to my Hungarian family. I really appreciate her contributions. My grandparents' escape from an oppressive government is a vivid example to me of how lucky I am to live in America.

Teaching at Belmont University has certainly challenged my authority on the subject of economics. I have interacted with scores of bright students and they have taught me a lesson or two through the years. A student's brilliant question can derail even the most well-planned lecture. I have also had the privilege of working with the numerous supportive individuals at the Massey Business School, both administratively and academically. They have made my teaching career such a wonderful experience.

I am also very lucky to work with the people at the Oakley Group. Not everyone is fortunate enough to truly enjoy the company of their coworkers inside and outside the office. Beverly Herbert, Sam Oakley, Jon Lockmiller, and Brian Dixon are all extremely talented and it has been a privilege to work alongside them. I always enjoy our discussions around economics and politics (as well as our weekly tennis match).

Many aspects of behavioral economics are value-based. I am blessed to have wonderful parents that continue to demonstrate to me the value of hard work and responsibility. My parents, Alex Vass Gal and Melda & Ed Colvin have been excellent role models. Through their love, support, discipline, and example, I have a strong moral foundation—one that continues to serve me well as obstacles arise.

My friends, family, and colleagues have all helped me so much. Simple dinner conversations, Facebook discussions, and other casual debates have all contributed to my various economic stances. I look forward to continuing to learn and grow from interactions with them in the future. I am extremely fortunate to be surrounded by brilliant people on a daily basis and am thankful for all of them.

www.ingramcontent.com/pod-product-compliance
Lightning Source LLC
Chambersburg PA
CBHW070111290526
45789CB00005B/2000